STUDIES IN AMERICAN HISTORY

III

BARBADOS

A STUDY OF

NORTH-AMERICAN-
WEST-INDIAN RELATIONS

1739-1789

BY

DAVID H. MAKINSON

1964

MOUTON & CO.

LONDON · THE HAGUE · PARIS

Printed in The Netherlands by Mouton & Co., Printers, The Hague

ACKNOWLEDGEMENTS

I wish to express my sincere appreciation to Professor Charles Gibson for his generous assistance and discerning counsel during the preparation of this work, and to Professor John Haefner for his concept of the program of which this paper is an integral part. I am also indebted to the officials of the Public Record Office, British Museum, West India Committee, and Society for the Propagation of the Gospel of the Church of England for their many kindnesses during several months of research.

Finally, I wish to express my gratitude to my wife for her encouragement and support.

CONTENTS

LIST OF ILLUSTRATIONS

INTRODUCTION

Prior to the eighteenth century an essential commerce had developed between the British colonies in North America and those in the West Indies based upon the desire and need of each for the products of the other. While this trade between the northern and tropical portions of the New World British Empire was but part of the vast and complex system of commercial activity emanating from Great Britain, and of less consequence to the mother country than her own commerce with either area, it formed the basis of much of the economic strength of the mainland colonies, and was considered so vital by the West Indian planters that its continuance was equated with their very survival.

However, by the fifth decade of the eighteenth century this economic relationship had become entangled in political and military questions relating to the international contest for supremacy then being waged between Great Britain and France, and would thereafter be increasingly affected by the course of political events ending in the American schism of 1783. While the events of the Seven Years' War and the American Revolution have often been narrated with regard to their obvious effect upon the American scene, much remains to be documented regarding the impact of these events in other parts of the British North American empire, particularly the West Indies.

Barbados in the eighteenth century was in many ways typical of the several British sugar colonies in the Caribbean, and a study of the island colony affords an insight into the effect of world events upon the British West Indies as a whole. The colony founded in the third decade of the seventeenth century, contemporary in age with the New England settlements of North America, had become, by virtue of its age and early development of the sugar industry, the acknowledged leader in economic and political affairs among the British islands of the Antilles. It is for this reason that a survey of Barbados among all of the British West India colonies is so rewarding.

Faced with a steadily declining economic and political position within the British Empire and an inability, caused in part by a lack of effective leadership, to correct the conditions responsible, most of the West Indians were obliged to remain bystanders to events which would lead to their own eventual economic disintegration.

American independence would finally rend apart the delicately balanced trade pattern within the empire which the British planters had strove so long to maintain and improve to their advantage. This decisive act would do much to accelerate the end of mercantilism and usher in the new trade policies inaugerated by Great Britain early in the nineteenth century. For mainland America was both a source of essential supply and the chief market for all of the Caribbean islands. In the years before mercantilism surrendered its primacy to the more modern economic policies of the nineteenth century, the success or failure of British arms in North America carried with it economic repercussions sufficient to annihilate dependent parts of the British Empire; so it was with Barbados and the other British Caribbean islands during the greater portion of the eighteenth century.

This book attempts to place in perspective those events of the period which affected the destiny of this prominent British West Indian colony, and by so doing trace the general course of affairs throughout the British Caribbean. Where appropriate, reference has been made to other colonies in an effort to enlarge the view and corroborate evidence. The narrative is one of a society physically isolated from its essential resources as well as the markets for its produce; a society which was seventy percent slave, and in which the greatest wealth and power was often absent from the island while the operation of vast holdings was left to salaried overseers. It is a history of a one-crop economy beset by the inefficiences of supervisory control, a poor and overworked soil, sudden and violent price fluctuations, foreign competion in world markets and even within the protected market of the empire itself, natural disasters both instantaneous and prolonged, and of risk in every facet of daily life.

Finally, it is the story of planter determination to protect the existing order against those forces which would undermine and destroy it, be they French, American rebels, wilful governors, harsh laws, political opponents in the colony and in London, or the unremitting passage of time. Their failure, indeed the impossibility of their task, must not be overlooked when recounting the full story of the British-French conflict in the New World and the events of the American Revolution.

I

THE SETTING FOR CONFLICT

The close of the seventeenth century was marked by the growing rivalry for world political and economic supremacy between the thrones of Great Britain and France. In the politics of Europe, in the commercial struggle of the Indian provinces, and in expansionist policies of both nations on the North American continent the battle was grimly waged. The expulsion of James II in 1688 and the accession of William and Mary to the English throne severed the last link in a centuries-old sorely-tried alliance between the two royal houses. The outbreak of hostilities the following year marked the beginning of a hundred and twenty-five years of sporadic warfare waged in every quarter of the globe, and not successfully concluded until the second decade of the nineteenth century. The eighteenth century witnessed a realignment of the two major kingdoms throughout the world, but submission of either one to the power of the other was to wait until Waterloo.

Perhaps nowhere in the world was the battle for supremacy more consistently waged, or the change of national fortune more readily apparent than in the Caribbean during the last six decades of the eighteenth century. The Antilles, originally under Spanish domination, had become by 1740 the arena for an economic and military struggle between France and Great Britain centered on a dozen small islands in the Leeward and Windward chains, and based upon the successful marketing of their chief export crops.

The uneasy peace following the Treaty of Utrecht had given both nations an opportunity to wage economic war upon one another for a quarter of a century. In the Indies the goal was the maintenance of one's own export market, coupled with its steady improvement at the expense of foreign competitors. From their two principal island bastions of Guadeloupe and Martinique the French carried out a relentless campaign of trade warfare aimed at undercutting the economic vitality of the British West Indian empire. They successfully breached the protective mercantile wall placed around the British colonies by the Acts of Trade and Navigation and were able to impede the growth of the British empire in the New World far more effectively through commercial competition than by military means.[1]

British West Indian settlement had begun in the third decade of the seventeenth century with the colonization of Barbados. In one hundred years over 5,000 square miles of island territory had come under British control. Barbados remained the "mother colony", having been continuously inhabited and cultivated since 1625.[2] All of the British islands had been acquired through settlement excepting Jamaica, captured from Spain in 1655, and several small islands in the Virgin group taken from the Netherlands during the second Dutch War.[3] The agricultural age of the British islands was a distinct disadvantage in the commercial rivalry with France, for the overworked soil of Barbados, Antigua, Nevis, and Montserrat had to vie with the fertility of the fresh soil on the large French islands.

Sugar with its related products, rum and molasses, was the principal crop of the Indies and the chief vehicle of the British-French economic and political struggle during the eighteenth century. A good crop coupled with a strong price in the export market assured the well-being of the planters, and a thriving local economy for another year. Any deviation from this pattern, regardless of cause, meant the disruption of the precarious equilibrium that was the insular sugar economy.

Profitable sugar production rested upon a double foundation of large tracts of cultivated acreage under one management, and sufficient cheap labor to perform the many tasks necessary for its proper cultivation. Long before the close of the seventeenth century the advantages of large scale sugar production had become apparent to French and British alike. The large producer could operate his refining plant more often and thus take fuller advantage of that fixed charge, he could purchase plantation supplies more cheaply because of the

[1] The colonization of Guadeloupe had taken place in 1635, and Martinique the same year. Their combined area is 1, 114 square miles.

[2] V. T. Harlow, *A History of Barbados, 1625-1685* (Oxford, 1926), p. 3. This date is disputed by several early writers who use 1605 as the year of first discovery, and by the Barbados government itself which celebrated the tercentary of the settlement of the island in 1927.

[3] Anegada and Virgin Gorda. Neither island figures prominently in Caribbean history.

larger quantities involved, and he could make more efficient use of his labor by rotating his planting schedule.[4]

On these small islands with a restricted amount of arable soil the acquisition of land by one planter meant a commensurate decrease in the amount of land available to other individuals; thus by 1700 practically all suitable land in the islands was under cultivation and the white population static or decreasing in numbers.[5] The system was characterized by large plantations, often managed by agents of an absentee owner, a one crop economy employing masses of slave labor, and the rigid adherence to proven agricultural methods, often well past the point of diminishing return.

The process of land acquisition continued throughout the seventeenth and eighteenth centuries, more slowly in times of large crops, favorable costs and selling prices, and at an accelerated pace in the poor market years and during wartime when increased expenses and high fixed costs often drove the small planter to the wall. By 1740 most of the British islands had taken on the characteristics of a two-level society. A decreasing group of planters, each owning more and more land as the years passed, was at the top of the social scale, while the majority of the remaining white residents were to be found in a broad lower class consisting of a few hired laborers, tradesmen, professional men, and the lesser grades of public servants.[6] A constant drain of men of talent and leadership from the older British islands was the inevitable result of a quiescent economy; a drain which left a void in the affairs of government that was never filled. The rigid application of inheritance by primogeniture throughout the islands offered little hope for the eventual breakup of the large estates through death, and actually served to intensify the tendency toward accumulation of land on the part of large planters.

The home government was aware of the faults of such a land system, but was unable to reverse the trend until the middle of the eighteenth century, and then with only limited success.[7] In an effort

[4] See D. H. Makinson, "A Survey of the Barbados Sugar Industry, 1642-1764", unpublished ms. (Iowa City, 1959), I, II, for a more detailed analysis of the operation of a sugar estate in the British West Indies.

[5] Jamaica affords us the exception. The island did not reach the zenith of its white population until early in the eighteenth century or achieve its greatest production until shortly before the American Revolution. The size and topography of the island explain in part, the slowness of its development.

[6] D. H. Makinson, *op. cit.*, p. 28.

[7] Lowell J. Ragatz, *The Fall of the Planter Class in the British Caribbean, 1763-1833* (London, 1928), pp. 38, 113, and D. H. Makinson, *op. cit.*, p. 38.

to retain the white population of the island the Barbados Assembly passed three acts prior to 1730 aimed at preventing white persons from leaving either involuntarily or on their own accord without just cause.[8] Acts of this sort were of little avail in attempting to halt the trend of island settlement, however.

Slave labor formed the basic unit of production on all the islands, regardless of ownership. There were Negroes working in the cane fields for British, French, Spanish, Dutch, and Danish masters, and the ratio of Negroes to whites on all of the islands soon became exceedingly high. This was another result of an agricultural system dependent upon one crop. In 1768 the official population figures for Barbados reveal 16,139 whites, 448 freed slaves and mulattoes, and 66,377 slaves.[9] These figures show a ratio that may be considered typical for the West Indies as a whole.

The danger of a slave revolt was always a real one, and the fear of an insurrection led to the passing of most of the laws aimed at maintaining the white population. Slave rebellions continued to be a major threat in the islands, for as long as the disparity in population existed armed Negroes could slaughter their masters and other whites within a few days time and with relative ease. Most planters felt that force, or the threat of it, must be met by force, thus any slave convicted of instigating or participating in a rebellion was sure to suffer death. The killing of a slave "with provocation" on Barbados was punishable only by a fine as late as the nineteenth century.[10]

The British slave trade had received its greatest impetus from the dealings of the Royal African Company which held a monopoly in the slaving trade from 1672 to 1697. While the company was beset by difficulties from the beginning and was continually on the edge of bankruptcy, it laid the foundation for a succesful private British slave trade in the eighteenth century.[11]

The slave trade has been the subject of much writing by students of history, and every child of twelve has been familiarized with the famous "three-cornered trade" between the West Indies, New England, and the west coast of Africa. Actually this was just one of several routes in existence during the period. Several of the British islands,

[8] *Calendar of State Papers,* (hereafter cited as *C.S.P.*), *1701,* No. 1183; *Ibid., 1724-25,* No. 751; *Ibid., 1726-27,* No. 189.

[9] See Table I.

[10] Harlow, *op. cit.,* p. 427n.

[11] Makinson, *op. cit.,* III, esp. pp. 40-45.

TABLE I

Population of Barbados for selected Years: 1748-1786

Year	White	Negro	Free Negro	Authority
1748	15,252	47,132	–	*C.O.* 318:2, no. 116.
1748	15,252	47,025	–	*C.O.* 29:28, Cc. 10.
1757	16,772	63,645	–	*C.O.* 28:31, Ee. 8; *C.O.* 318:2, no. 116.
1762	18,419	–	–	*C.O.* 28:55, nos. 78-94.
1762	18,419	70,000	–	*C.O.* 28:32, Ff. 25.
1768	16,139	66,827	–	*C.O.* 318:2, no. 116.
1768	–	76,275	–	*C.O.* 31:34.
1768	16,139	66,377	488	*C.O.* 28:33, Gg. 27.
1772	–	74,485	–	*C.O.* 31:34.
1773	18,532	68,548	534	*C.O.* 318:2, no. 116.
1773	18,532	68,908	–	*C.O.* 318:2, no. 19.
1783	16,167	58,275	–	*C.O.* 318:2, no. 116.
1783	16,167	57,434	838	*C.O.* 318:2, no. 21; *C.O.* 28:42.
1786	16,167	52,115	838	Edwards, *op. cit.*, p. 346.

notably Barbados, became intermediate distribution points for new Negroes brought over from Africa.

In the second decade of the eighteenth century Barbados began to serve as a center of operations for persons selling slaves to the French, as the French on Guadeloupe, St. Lucia, and Martinique were working diligently to bring these island into full production, and their need for new labor was pressing. The re-exportation of slaves from Barbados continued throughout the century, uninterrupted by changes in the economic or political climate. Many of the Negroes consigned to Barbados by the Royal Africa Company for local use were re-exported to the French islands at a handsome profit. Another source of supply was the debt-ridden planters who often sold their slaves to a Barbados broker before fleeing the island and their creditors.[12]

The slave trade with the Dutch and the French was only part of a much larger trade in sugar, provisions and manufactured articles which was carried on throughout most of the eighteenth century, and which became the active concern of the British government at home and its representatives in the islands. In spite of laws and other

[12] *C.S.P. Col.*, 1719-20, Nos. 356 II, 388; *Ibid. 1734-35,* No. 376 II.

measures designed to control this trade, the slave phase was limited only by the number of Negroes available at any one time and the demands of the island planters.[13]

During the war years between 1739 and 1763 the movement of slaves between the islands continued strong. Governor Robinson of Barbados reported to the Board of Trade in 1742 that the trade between Barbados and the French islands was greater than ever before, in spite of the outbreak of the Spanish war three years previously. He stated that buyers from Martinique were openly coming to Barbados and dealing directly with the local planters. Terms of sale were cash, or hard-to-obtain merchandise such as "soap, wax-candles, wine, gold and silver, brocades, and laces". Robinson noted that his share of customs seizures had not exceeded the ridiculously low figure of seven pounds sterling per year for seven years, and pleaded to know, "what are the Officers of the Customs doing to tolerate these things?"[14] Trade was vital to the survival of the islands at any time, but particularly so in time of war when the normal trade channels were apt to be disrupted. Political differences became unimportant when economic survival was at stake.

Much has been written about the treatment of slaves by the planters and on the practice of slavery itself. But philosophical arguments aside it should not be too difficult to prove that the imported Negro in the West Indies enjoyed a better material existence than he had had in Africa. It is even possible that the plantation laborers' standard of living might well have aroused the envy of most of the eighteenth century European peasantry – including the British.[15]

The economic survival of each of the islands depended upon success in the profitable marketing of locally produced sugar, and individuals and governments always strove toward this goal. Though often working at cross-purposes, their aims were identical: the promotion of their own and their island's welfare; only secondly was the well-being of the mother country encouraged. When we consider the insular positions of these possessions, their monocultural system of agriculture, their homogeneous planter populations, and the great distance in miles and time between the Caribbean and the capitals of Europe it is easy to understand this lack of regard for the problems

[13] Makinson, *op. cit.*, p. 47.

[14] Original manuscript, Public Record Office, Chancery Lane, London, W.C.2. *Colonial Office Papers* (hereafter indicated as *C.O.*), 28:26, Bb. 1.

[15] Ragatz, *op. cit.*, p. 27.

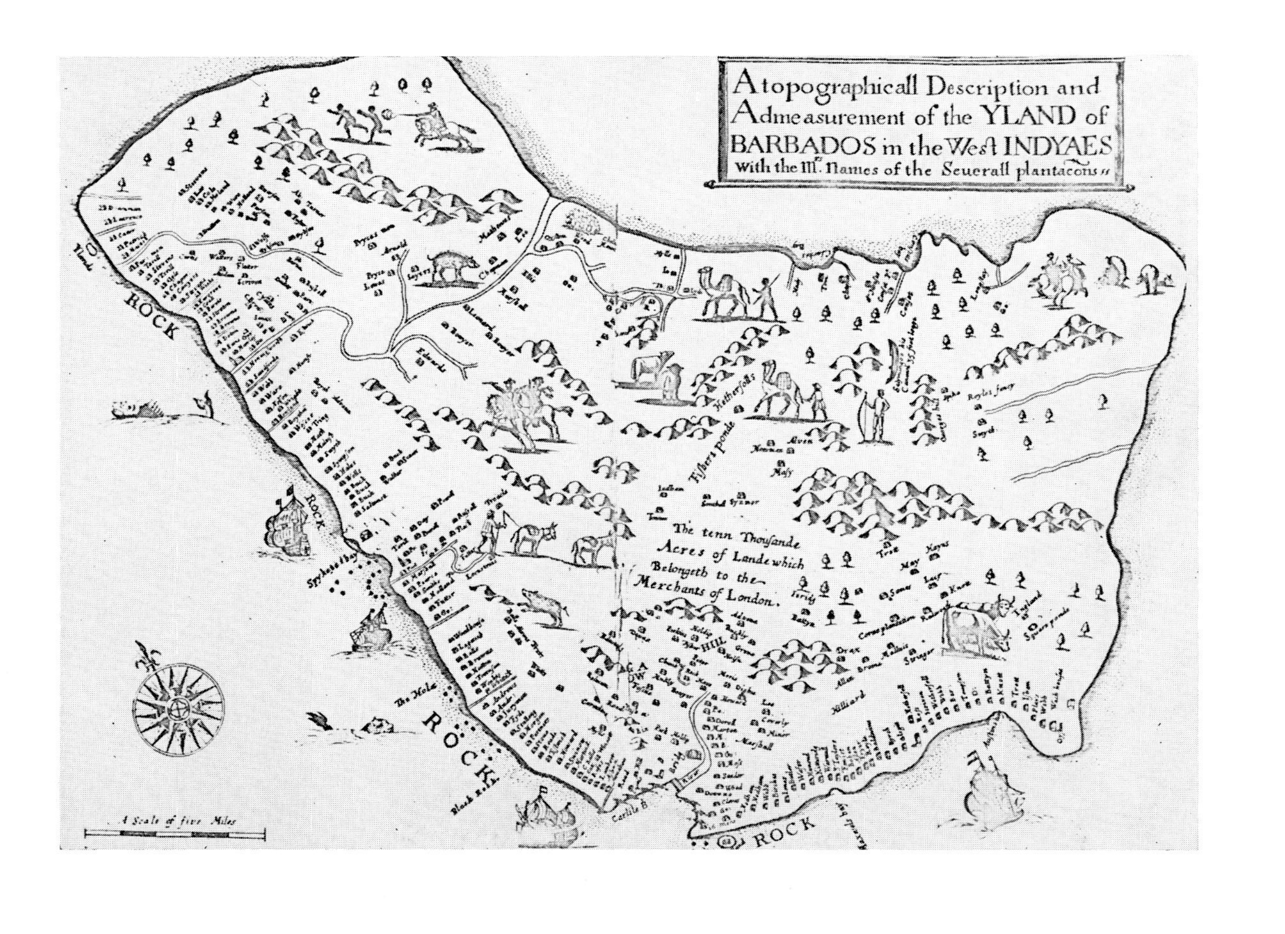
Atopographicall Description and
Admeasurement of the YLAND of
BARBADOS in the West INDYAES
with the Mrs. Names of the Seuerall plantacons
The tenn Thousande
Acres of Lande which
Belongeth to the
Merchants of London.
Fysshers ponde
ROCK
ROCK
ROCK
ROCK
ROCK
Spyketes bay
The Hole
Carlile B.
A Scale of five Miles

of imperial administration. The motivation behind various schemes, restrictions, and commercial devices used to promote island welfare may also be more readily grasped in view of the unusual circumstances surrounding their inception.

As the eighteenth century progressed and economic competition became more intense, the British planters likewise increased their efforts to achieve some type of economic advantage for their exports. These efforts took two distinct forms: one was a series of petitions to the Council of Trade and Plantations and the monarch for relief within the framework of the Navigation Acts; the other was the development and promotion of a clandestine trade in sugar, slaves, provisions, and other commodities carried on outside the legal limits of the acts.[16] Both methods were to some degree effective in granting relief and could be defended on the grounds of expediency alone during much of the century.

Probably the most striking phenomena of the relationship between Britain and her colonies were the strength of the West Indian sugar lobby in Parliament and the lengths to which Britain was willing to go to preserve the economic health of her sugar colonies. It can be said that the West Indian planters were never satisfied with their economic situation as long as they could devise a new way to improve their position, even at the expense of others. That sometimes the devices which they sought and used placed additional burdens on other Englishmen was of little concern to the planters and their merchant allies.[17]

Nonetheless, the British planters were forced to offer their products for sale handicapped by regulations, restrictions, and taxes much more confining and severe than any imposed upon their foreign competitors. Within the empire the Leeward Island sugar producers, notably the Barbados planters, were forced to carry an additional tax burden of $4\frac{1}{2}$ percent levied on the value of "all dead commodities of the growth or produce of (the) island, that shall be shipped off the same".[18] This duty dating back to 1663 and arising from the recognition by Charles II of the Barbadian planters' land titles, many of which were of a doubtful nature owing to the muddled estate of the original proprietor, remained a financial millstone around the necks

[16] Makinson, *op. cit.*, p. 59.

[17] *Idem.*

[18] An act for settling the Import on the Commodities of the Growth of this Island. Passed 12 September 1663, Barbados Assembly, No. 36. From Sir Alan Burns, *History of the British West Indies* (London, 1954), p. 132.

of the Barbadians for 175 years.[19] It was not removed until 1838.

Using the first course of action in an effort to improve their relative position, the planters resorted to numerous petitions to the home government, each drawn up and presented by a legislature of the islands and usually presented to the recipient by an agent of the colony residing in London. The West Indians used every possible approach in attempting to display their economic plight. Like hurt children seeking succor from an understanding parent they poured forth their grievances to their monarch and Parliament in one petition after another, each one more plaintive and garrulous the the last.

To illustrate the growing weakness of their competitive position in the production of sugar, even within the commonwealth, planters on the older islands (Antigua and Barbados) complained of the increasing sterility of their soil. Here was a legitimate handicap, but one scarcely amenable to relief from Whitehall. The productiveness of the recently planted soils in the French islands and in the newer British colonies – more notably Jamaica – could not be disputed, nor could it be denied that the soil of the older islands was giving out for lack of proper management. Among the planters thus handicapped it was felt that the answer lay in some sort of tariff protection or tax relief for their products in order to create an artificial equalization among all sugars in the home market.

Another approach used in seeking relief was to cite the importance of the sugar islands to Britain and the rest of the empire by reminders of the large number of individuals and businesses that were dependent upon a healthy sugar economy. If the desired results were not always obtained from the king or Parliament the occasional publication of petitions or other tracts favorable to the West Indies by island agents or retired planters in England served to sharpen the awareness of many merchants, shipowners, and investors of their vested interest in a robust sugar economy.[20] Neither did the businessmen engaged

[19] The tax arose out the settlement of the claims of the heirs and creditors of the second Earl of Carlisle by the king. The agreement provided for the recognition by the crown of the titles to lands owned by the Barbadians, and the abolition of the dues and rents formerly paid to the proprietor, in return for the tax on exports.

[20] Perhaps the best example of partisan writing in the guise of historical research is Bryan Edwards', *The History, Civil and Commercial of the British Colonies in the West Indies* (London, 1793). This two volume history which ran through five editions by 1819 was written by Edwards, long a resident of Jamaica, in an attempt to present the West Indian case in the controversy then raging over trade with the United States and the treatment of the Negro slave.

in the sugar trade need to be reminded often of the source of their profits, nor were they, as a group, reticent about expressing their great admiration for the planters and their desire to be of service to them in group efforts for economic gain.[21]

It was not, however, through any drastic changes in the Acts of Trade that the West Indian planters were to achieve their greatest successes in their economic war. The greatest gains were made by a constant struggle to stifle any trade by other members of the Commonwealth that would benefit, even indirectly, their foreign competitors, and to retard or stop further economic expansion by French and Dutch interests. In this direction the planters continued to be successful to the degree that their influence in Parliament was sufficiently strong to overcome the opposition.

Their first success came in 1699 when the Lords of Trade refused to authorize the colonizing of the island of Tobago on the grounds that such a settlement would be prejudicial to the trade of Barbados and the other sugar islands in the Leewards.[22] This action by the Lords marked the beginning of a series of favorable decisions affecting the sugar industry, and it signaled the start of the future sugar lobby in England.

But the threat of competition remained acute to the planters of the older islands, particularly Barbados. By 1710 traders from the British North American colonies had become the foremost suppliers of provisions to the British West Indies and had also begun to wax prosperous from the trade; perhaps a little too prosperous in the eyes of the Barbadians. The North Americans offered flour, lumber, grain, horses, casks, and a host of other items sorely needed by the planters, and took in exchange sugar, indigo, rum, and molasses. Since it was no secret that many of the newer islands were able to produce more sugar per acre, and at a lower cost, than could Barbados it was natural to expect the northern traders to do much of their exchanging with these islands.

Here was a grave threat to Barbados, far more serious than high taxes or trade restrictions, for Barbados had long since lost her leading position in the field of sugar production, and she was now losing it in the sales field, even within the empire. If it seemed unfair for Englishmen to profit at the expense of other Englishmen, it seemed

[21] A good example of concerted action between planter and merchant occurred in 1731 when the Liverpool merchants trading with Barbados supported a petition from the planters asking for free trade. *C.S.P., Col., 1731,* No. 39 II.

[22] *Ibid., 1699,* No. 420. After a hundred years of disputed status Tobago was formally ceded to Great Britain by the Treaty of Paris in 1764.

doubly unfair when the transactions aided foreigners in their economic struggles against fellow countrymen.[23] Protests were lodged as early as 1710 against the "New England" trade with the foreign sugar islands, and ending this, plus renewed efforts for free trade in sugar unrestricted by the Navigation Acts, became the foremost objectives of the Barbados planters for the next one hundred years.[24]

The period from the end of the War of Spanish Succession to 1730 saw a remarkable expansion in sugar consumption in Britain and with it a rise in the selling price. The increased demand for sugar in both Britain and continental Europe caused by the widespread use of coffee for the first time created a market in the 1720's for even the relatively high-priced Barbados sugars. The prosperity of the twenties temporarily halted the flow of petitions concerning sugar. Only British rum and molasses continued to suffer from French competition.

The French planters lacked a home market for rum in wine-drinking France, and by selling to the mainland colonists through the years at consistently low prices had been able to dispose of most of their molasses at a profit. Jamaican rum was assured of a steady market among the middle and upper classes in Britain and North America owing to its reputation for superior quality. This left Barbadian rum in direct competition with that produced in New England from French and Dutch molasses.

Governor Worsley of Barbados complained in 1724 that New England trade with the French islands and rum manufacture in North America had cut the price of Barbados rum in half.[25] A Philadelphia merchant probably best expressed the sentiments of most of the mainland colonists regarding the use of foreign molasses when he stated that:

> the Surinam trade will live when our islanders may starve for the Dutch neither use their molasses nor their rum, save what they give to their negroes but we are their only customers for molasses & of late rum, considerable quantities come from thence, they take to grinding their

[23] Makinson, *op. cit.*, pp. 93-94.

[24] *Idem.* The Barbadians did not fight the battle alone. By 1730 the legislatures of most of the islands had petitioned the home government for action against the increased volume of American-French trade. By 1765 several colonies had been successful in securing free ports for themselves.

[25] *C.S.P. Col., 1724-25*, No. 832 V. Richard Pares, *Yankees and Creoles* (Cambridge, 1956), pp. 29-36, states that the New England distilling industry was well developed around Boston by the start of the eighteenth century, and that by 1720 New York, Philadelphia, and several small towns in Massachusetts contained distilleries for the production of rum from West Indian molasses.

damaged canes & work it up & sell it for about 6d. per gallon. . . . . We purchase a whole load there up here at 40/– and 50/– per head and half a score such may load a sloop as big as my sloop Mary . . .[26]

So much foreign rum was carried to North America by the mainland traders that the price remained depressed until the renewal of warfare in the Caribbean in 1739.[27]

The high price of sugar began to fall by 1728 when the British market became temporarily oversupplied because of increased production and a succession of bumper harvests in the West Indies. Once again the volume of complaints rose inversely with the drop in prices. Some official concern was expressed at this time, and inquiry into the question of prices by the Council of Trade served to highlight the inroads then being made by French and Dutch sugars on the British market.[28]

After a comprehensive study of the state of the sugar trade had been made, the Council's report reflected a serious concern for the future of the British sugar islands if positive steps were not taken to restore British sugars to worldwide competition. In a lucid argument for continued trade with the foreign sugar islands rather than the enactment of new trade restrictions, the Council asked

> whether it may not be advisable to connive at this trade and carry the French sugars for them to foreign markets, rather than let them be carriers themselves; and so much the better, because by this trade the Northern Colonies upon the continent are probably enabled to pay the balance which they yearly owe to Great Britain, not having commodities of their own produce to exchange against these they receive from us.[29]

For the first time the Council had not taken a negative stand on the question of free trade.[30]

As trade conditions grew steadily worse and the price of sugar remained depressed on the London market the West Indians petitioned the king to: (1) require all foreign produce intended for sale within

[26] Jonathan Dickinson to Issac Gale, May 1721. The Letter Book of Jonathan Dickinson, p. 370, Library Company of Philadelphia. Cited in *Ibid.*, p. 51.

[27] *Ibid.*, p. 127.

[28] Specific figures may be noted in Makinson, *op. cit.*, p. 102.

[29] *Ibid.*, pp. 102-103 from *C.S.P. Col., 1724-25,* No. 291.

[30] Previous Council of Trade decisions affecting the sale and transportation of sugar had always supported the mercantile theories inherent in the restrictive features of the Acts of Trade. This statement reflects the growing feeling among responsible officials that some modifications in the Acts might be necessary for the full development of many parts of the expanding British empire.

the empire to go through England and pay duties upon import and re-export; (2) forbid direct importation of foreign products by Ireland; (3) allow free trade between the English planters and all foreign ports, "as foreigners now have with England paying only one percent upon export".[31]

The commercial rivalry with France was never more keen, and the constant stream of provisions sent to the French and Dutch islands by the northern colonists compounded the already grave injury done to the British planting interests by those nations. Many planters who operated on a narrow profit margin and were barely solvent during the good years of the previous decade were ruined by the price decline. Often the bankrupt planters fled their estates and island with their slaves and other moveable property a jump ahead of their creditors creating further financial havoc in the colonies.[32]

American reaction to the West Indian proposals was immediate and vehement. The London agents of many of the North American colonies protested that the proposals, if placed in effect, would ruin the economy of their respective areas.[33] The Board of Trade was aware of the divergent interests of its American colonies and that any action taken by the home government would be apt to cause injury to one or more special interest group. The Board adopted the policy of hearing evidence both supporting and opposing changes in the existing Acts, and upon the close of the hearings referred the matter to Parliament.

After prolonged debate in Commons and in the House of Lords, several of the planter suggestions were embodied in the Molasses Act of 1733. The act did not prohibit trade between the northern colonies and foreign plantations, but rather levied prohibitive import duties on the French sugar, molasses, and rum.[34] This partial victory of the sugar interests, led by the Barbadians, while not complete, was significant, and reflected the growing power of the West Indians in Parliament.

[31] *C.S.P. Col., 1730,* No. 549 I.

[32] F. W. Pitman, *The Development of the British West Indies, 1700-1763* (New Haven, 1917), p. 134. It was during the 1730's that several schemes for aiding bankrupts were put forth by the island residents. Most notable of these was that of the Barbados planter, John Ashley, who promoted a plan in 1737 for operating the estates of insolvent planters under receiverships. See *C.O.* 28:25.

[33] *C.S.P. Col., 1730,* No. 549 III, IV, V.

[34] 9d. on each gallon of rum, 6d. per gallon of molasses, and 5s. per hundredweight of sugar, collected upon unloading at the port of entry.

The effect on prices was instantaneous. Muscovado rose to 25 s. in 1734, a rise of 8 s. from the previous year.[35] However, the increase in price was short-lived; by 1735 the average price had fallen to within two shillings of its previous low, and the news that the northern colonists were evading the act with impunity left little hope that the situation might soon improve. Even if the act had been obeyed, there were many who felt that more stringent measures were necessary before British sugar could become competitive on the world market.

Underlying all of the official efforts to promote the economies of the various British islands was the clandestine trade of the island merchants and planters that had been flourishing as an integral part of the Caribbean economic life since European settlement first began in the sixteenth century. During the troubled eighteenth century this trade had reached new heights in volume, especially during the war years when normal trade channels were liable to be disrupted. Indeed the Acts of Trade had been evaded from their inception to a degree dependent directly upon their restrictiveness on the West Indian planters and their merchant allies in North America and the mother country.

This iniquitous trade ranged from the bribing of customs officials to overlook cargoes, through falsification of papers, to trading with the enemy in wartime. Records of smuggling activities and other illegal trading are difficult to obtain, primarily because few were kept. Still, from the volume of complaints that was issued, and the expense and time devoted to controlling these activities we can glean the impression that they must have been considerable over a long period of time.

The bribing of customs officials constituted perhaps the chief form of violation practised by most of the West Indian merchants. The underpaid and underprivileged public servants were usually most tractable when properly recompensed for their lack of diligence on the docks, and illegal cargo usually flowed freely through most West Indian ports. The occasional honest customs collector was apt to find himself extremely unpopular with the local populace. One Barbadian

[35] Muscovado was the golden colored (brown) sugar that formed the bulk of the world's sugar supply. A more highly refined type called clayed (white) sugar, was also produced and commanded a much higher price during the seventeenth and eighteenth centuries. Although improved refining methods continued to lower its cost throughout the 1700's, clayed sugar never captured more than fifteen percent of the British market.

collector stated that numerous threats had been made against him for doing his duty too diligently![36]

It is interesting to note that use of bribes enabled the planters to carry on a limited trade with Europe thus evading the prohibition against it found in the Acts. The method employed was to conceal a variety of merchandise underneath a cargo of staple items on which the various duties would be paid. By loading and unloading in one of the smaller English ports, thus following the requirement that all goods must first stop in England, such as Falmouth or Dover and bribing the customs officials, vast quantities of goods were freely exchanged between Europe and the West Indies.

If it was not possible to control the customs inspectors in a port in the West Indies, contraband merchandise could be landed in the outlying bays and creeks of most islands in order to avoid the payment of duties. Many captains simply unloaded outside the harbor when a suitable anchorage could not be found elsewhere. By using small boats to convey the cargo to the shore, usually at night, merchandise could be landed at several places along the beach and carried directly to one or more estates by wagon before morning.

The frequent wars of the period, that disrupted the normal channels of commerce, served to increase the dependence of the island residents on these interlopers, and even gave them an aura of respectability granted only to those individuals who had the power to save an island from isolation and starvation.[37]

One of the most profitable forms of outside trade was carried on with Spanish merchants from the South American mainland, Cuba, Santo Domingo, and Puerto Rico. Although this trade was prohibited to varying degrees by the Acts and in its entirety by the Spanish government, it had reached sizeable proportions by the early eighteenth century. On Barbados excess slaves were traded for gold coin, machinery, and provisions from the Spanish settlements on the South American coast during the War of Spanish Succession even though Britain and Spain were enemies.

It was Spanish gold that enabled the Barbadians to continue their purchases of badly needed provisions from the North American traders.[38] For it was the northern colonists who played the role of chief purveyors in this unofficial traffic between the West Indians

[36] *C.S.P. Col., 1699,* No. 476.
[37] Makinson, *op. cit.,* p. 82.
[38] *C.S.P. Col., 1706-08,* No. 1591; *Ibid., 1708-09,* No. 134.

and those with whom they traded. And by the eighteenth century many American merchants preferred to purchase the lower-priced French and Dutch sugars with cash earned in the British islands than to make less profit carrying British sugar home to Boston or Philadelphia. The newer islands were able to produce sugar so cheaply that it became common practice for merchants on Barbados to import sugar from these islands and then market it through the regular trade channels as Barbados grown. This was often done with Dutch sugar from Surinam. So much foreign sugar consistently entered Barbados in the eighteenth century that its importation was a constant threat to the solvency of those planters who relied on marketing only the locally produced crop.

In the matter of economic survival nationalities ceased to be of importance; while British soldiers from the homeland and the northern colonies fought the French across the snow-covered forests of Nova Scotia, their fellow countrymen might be simultaneously concluding negotiations in the Caribbean for any of scores of products freely traded between the two enemies.

International rivalries and tensions were freely subordinated to parochial economic interests by British and French planters alike – even in the midst of open warfare between the two nations. Trading was made somewhat more difficult by being in the proximity of the fighting, and made easier in direct proportion to the distance between the islands and the battle area. Thus heavy fighting on the North American continent did little to impede the flow of supplies throughout the Caribbean.

Much of the indifference with which the British planters viewed their role in the imperial design could be directly traced to their view of themselves as residents of the islands. It was not unusual for the British planter to look upon himself as a transplanted Englishman, as indeed he often was. For it was common to consider residence in the Caribbean as only a temporary thing. Children of wealthy planters were invariably sent to England for their formal schooling, and it was not uncommon for planters and merchants to maintain residences both in the islands and in Britain.

Here we note an important contrast with the northern colonies. No matter how pleasurable and profitable tropical island living might have been, it did not become a substitute for the temperate climate of the mother country in the eyes of most British settlers. That is, it was difficult to become completely acclimatized in such a radically different environment. In North America the English and Scotch settlers could, and did, find areas in the vast expanse of new land that were not unlike their former homes. It was easy for many to estabish a new allegiance to a land so similar to the mother country and yet so full of promise.

The Indies too, were a place of opportunity – but nothing more. The islands had originally been a quick way to a fortune, if you were industrious and had several good years without drought or a hurricane. But by the eighteenth century that opportunity had gradually faded away as the once-new lands lost their productiveness to repeated plantings of a single crop, and slave labor gradually replaced free labor in the trades and crafts.

This was an alien society based upon profit and forced to rely on masses of slave labor for its proper functioning. Competing in world markets hampered, hindered, aided, and assisted by a series of complicated and ever-changing laws enacted by country squires, bishops, and businessmen, five thousand miles and two months away, the planters evolved their own little society apart from both their fellow countrymen to the north and those at home. Nonetheless, the West Indian did not identify himself so completely with his culture that he lost his former identity; indeed, he never did; he could not.

We can perhaps consider the British West Indies as a sub-society within the framework of the British tradition. It contained a homogeneous class of landed whites directing an exotic economy and which never established the affinity with the land that had been the hallmark of the British gentry for centuries.[39] These islands were the outposts of an empire whose function, in addition to their own betterment, was the promotion of the mother country and its institutions in all times.

The planter, be he second or third generation island born, was more British than West Indian in his views of empire, for his remoteness was the very thing that caused him to seek the protection of the British state. Troubled as he might have been by the inequities of the Acts of Trade, and though he might circumvent the law when it was to his benefit, he was made painfully aware of his total dependence upon the parent state by the frequent wars of the period. For without assistance from home there would be no trade, without trade only the prospect of starvation and ruin.

[39] A parallel case in point might be that of the British role in India during the eighteenth and nineteenth centuries.

With the possible exception of Jamaica, the West Indies were not self-sufficient. Most of the smaller islands had been planted to sugar for generations, and while some diversity in planting was to be found in the former "neutral islands" after 1763, it had always been easier and cheaper to import the necessary foodstuffs from North America and Britain than to use precious acreage for food production. This condition made the West Indian utterly dependent upon outside support for the proper functioning of his economy; it was basic to all other considerations involving his well-being.

Throughout the century an inconsistency of motive is apparent in the actions of the planters as they chaffed at restraints imposed by the home government, while simultaneously urging that a greater interest be taken in other aspects of their affairs by that same institution. The planter was a victim of his environment in a literal sense: tied to one, or a few cash crops, dependent upon distant markets that he could not control and agents whose ability and honesty he could not ascertain, physically isolated from the source of his law, provisions, and material, at the mercy of the capricious tropical elements, and pressed down by the knowledge that the time of opportunity had indeed departed, he continued to follow the course of existence established by his predecessors, hoping with a gambler's hope that somehow he might be able to extricate himself from debt, responsibility, and fear.

It has been argued that the planters were "the conspicuously rich men of Great Britain in the middle of the seventeen hundreds" and that with this wealth were able to exercise inordinate power over the course of events.[40] While we can document the existence of a strong sugar lobby and its effectiveness on numerous occasions in promoting the sugar interests, its existence was not necessarily the manifestation of a healthy sugar economy in the British West Indies. Political power is very often hard to obtain and usually obtainable only through years of effort. Once entrenched, such power is equally difficult to dissipate and is often held by interests mortally weakened from within. Such was the status of the West Indian planters by 1740.

Wealth created from sugar lacked a rational foundation. It was artificial, resting upon a paper monopoly secured by the much-abused Acts of Trade, and doomed to destruction at the hands of nature, competitors, and the inherent inefficiency of a wasteful system of production and distribution.

[40] Ragatz, *op. cit.*, p. vii.

Conditions of economic and political life had changed in the West Indies from the settlement years of the seventeenth century. By the fifth decade of the eighteenth century the old order of things had been badly strained by new economic pressures unknown only a generation earlier. Revisions and alterations were needed to shore up the faltering West Indian economy, and when, instead, the old doctrines continued to be used, the eventual loss of the Caribbean colonies as an effective source of British influence in America was to be expected. This same lack of insight in colonial affairs brought about an eventual rupture between Great Britain and her northern colonies, and in the Caribbean the neutralization in fact, if not in spirit, of the British islands during the War for American Independence.

II

THE FRENCH MENACE

The artificial attempt to control the empire sugar market by the Molasses Act of 1733 soon failed amid incessant North American trade with the French and Dutch sugar islands. While the British islands continued to receive provisions and supplies from their fellow colonists to the North, trade was usually conducted on a cash basis, thus continuing the drain of hard currency from the already impoverished colonies.

A memorialist of the period offered an accurate description of the abuse the Molasses Act was receiving at the hands of the North American colonists:

> I am sorry to observe that the duties imposed thereby on foreign rum and molasses are evaded, and the design of that well intended law totally eluded. . . . Tis notorious that most of the Northern Traders who come hither to the L.I., do now sell their cargoes, or such part thereof, as is most in demand, for ready money. This they carry off and rendezvous sometimes 40 sail at a time at St. Eustatia, where great quantities of the commodities I'm speaking of, are constantly lodged for sale.[1]

The islands languished amid depressed prices on the London sugar market and the intense foreign competition fraudulenty carried on within the empire. In 1737 Governor William Mathew of Antigua wrote of the plight of that colony and stated, "Indeed I never saw the condition of the sugar planters reduced so low, even to indigence, tho for thirty years I have been concerned here."[2] James Dottin, President of the Barbados Council wrote of the difficulty of collecting the $4\frac{1}{2}$ percent tax owing to the depressed state of trade.[3] Even Jamaica with its relatively fresh soil had been hardpressed by the

[1] T. Osborne, *Caribbeana, Letters and Dissertations* (London, 1741), II, pp. 129-132.

[2] Governor William Mathew to the Duke of Newcastle, 17 January 1737. *C.O.* 152:44, fos. 87-88d.

[3] Dottin to the Board of Trade, 14 May 1737. C.O. 28:25; AA. 64.

"excessive fall' in the price of sugar in Great Britain, "the sole mart allowed" for its marketing.[4]

Adding to the economic burden borne by the planters were several serious slave revolts in the thirties, the most dangerous occurring in Jamaica in 1736, and lasting several years. By fleeing into the mountainous interior several bands of armed slaves were able to menace wide areas of the island with relative impunity, and keep at bay forces far superior in strength for a number of years.[5]

Overriding these domestic issues in importance was the growing menace of French power in the Antilles. For over twenty years the French had been working to improve their military position in anticipation of an eventual renewal of warfare in the Caribbean. Their key to power was the possession of islands from which to launch attacks upon the enemy and from which defenses could be erected to thwart possible counter-attacks on Martinique and Guadeloupe. The Treaty of Utrecht had specified the neutralization of several of the West Indian islands whose ownership was in doubt owing to conflicting claims by both France and Great Britain, and it was in these islands that France soon began surreptitiously to spread her control.

The chief targets of this movement were the remaining large islands in the chain comprising the Lesser Antilles. This group of loosely arranged islands stretching over six hundred miles from Anquilla in the North to Trinidad at the mouth of the Orinoco River had always been the center of French West Indian activity since the colonization of Guadeloupe and Martinique in the previous century. The northernmost islands of the chain had been settled by the British and Dutch and with Barbados, these British colonies had become the nucleus of that country's early sugar empire.

The area that was to feel the pressure of French expansionist movement lay down the center spine of the Lesser Antilles from Guadeloupe to Grenada, which included the six largest islands of the chain. Martinique and Guadeloupe had been French for one hundred years, and Grenada a colony since 1650. It was into the vacuum

[4] President Gregory to the Duke of Newcastle, 23 November 1736. C.O. 137:22, fos. 101-102.

[5] There is some question whether this revolt and several later ones were ever put down. Since so many slaves continually fled to the interior of the island large parts of Jamaica, nominally controlled by the whites, were, in fact, the undisputed domain of bands of escaped and armed Negroes quite able to repulse any attack on their territory. See, *Idem.*

created by the conflicting claims to Dominica, St. Lucia, and St.Vincent that the French moved. These islands were largely uninhabited by Europeans, in part due to the question of ownership, and in part due to the fierce resistance of the native Caribs who were consistently hostile in their contacts with interlopers. Carib hostility was particularly strong on Dominica and St. Vincent where several seventeenth-century settlement attempts by both English and French planters ended in failure.

By the 1730's however the French had had some success in establishing a few scattered settlements on all three islands. By using the same tactics that had worked so well in Canada they had managed to get several small plantations into production and to garrison portions of the island with troops. The French made no overt effort to subvert Carib authority, preferring instead to move in amongst the natives offering rum, hardware, and technical skill in return for their safety. Dominica and St. Vincent also harbored large groups of Negro slaves who had escaped from the adjacent islands, and who were continually at war with the Caribs, or, at best, existed in a state of armed neutrality. The French were often successful in playing one group against the other to their own advantage, and on Dominica succeeded in decimating both groups by fostering Negro-Carib antagonisms while remaining ostensively uninvolved.

The British planters viewed the French movements with alarm; not only were the French settlements evidence of a deliberate violation of the treaty provisions insuring the islands' continued neutrality and evacuation, but successful French occupation meant futher sugar competition in peace and a threat to British sovereignty in wartime. Antigua, lying only fifty miles from Guadeloupe, was particularly vulnerable to strong attack, and in 1737 its London agent was directed to ask for more soldiers to be sent out to reinforce its tiny garrison. He reported that the planters were fearful of a renewal of hostilities with the French and were afraid of a slave uprising on the islands in case of a French attack. With 24,000 Negroes and only 3,000 whites on Antigua this fear might not have been without foundation.[6]

Among the Barbadians fear also ran high that the French activity on St. Lucia and St. Vincent meant an eventual armed attack on Barbados using the two "neutral islands" as spring-boards. Upon the

[6] Petition of John Yeomans, agent for Antigua, before 21 February 1737. *C.O.* 152:40, fos. 288b. 288c.

death of Governor Howe in 1736, the affairs of government passed to James Dottin, President of the Council, who, as a large landowner, was immediately concerned for the safety of the island. Always alert for signs of increased French activity, he found ample proof of a French build-up during the three years of his de facto rule and so informed his superiors at home.

As the threat of a new rupture between Britain and France increased, Dottin's alarm grew commensurately. In 1738 he informed the Board of Trade of a continual increase in the number of French settlers on St. Lucia in violation of the treaty for evacuating the island, and somewhat ruefully stated that "it was a mistaken policy" to have allowed the French to have seized the island in the first place.[7] He lamented the state of the fortifications protecting Barbados which were always in a state of disrepair owing to the habitual reluctance of the Assembly to allocate funds for their maintenance and restoration.[8] He further commented on the sorry economic plight of the island's inhabitants by stating that the island was becoming depopulated as "estates broke up and destroyed and (a) a number of the Planters continue in debt, and have little of their own to lose; I believe the resistance the Enemy would meet with would not be so warm and vigorous as I could wish . . .".[9]

Dottin continued to express his alarm over the French activities in an effort to incite some sort of action from the home government. Although Barbados had never been attacked during the two previous wars with France, its residents were keenly aware of the island's isolated position with respect to the rest of the Antilles, and were sensitive to the weakness of their defenses. A two-sided approach to the menance of France was used in official correspondence with the

[7] James Dottin, President of Council, to the Board of Trade, 4 November 1738. *C.O.* 28:25, Aa. 72.

[8] This was a constant complaint of Barbadian governors since the passage of the 4½ percent duty in 1663. While the proceeds from this tax were usually used for various purposes from enhancing the king's personal wealth to pensions for favored persons, the Assemblies always contended (not without foundation) that most of the funds were designated by the terms of the original agreement for the island's defense. They were thus always extremely reluctant to vote for the spending of local tax moneys on what was, to them, the responsibility of the Board of Trade. Fortunately for both sides in the argument the island's fortifications were never put to the test, since Barbados remained the only British island in the Antilles never attacked by an enemy fleet throughout the long era of British and French conflict from 1689 to 1815.

[9] Dottin to Board of Trade, 4 November 1738. *C.O.* 28:25, Aa. 72.

Board: the military threat posed to British security by French expansion, and the economic threat to the British sugar market occasioned by increased French sugar production from the neutral islands.

Pleas for warships to defend Barbados from possible attack,[10] and reminders of the commercial value of the neutral islands fill the correspondence of the period. In 1739 Dottin again complained of the presence of the French on St. Lucia, and reminded the Board that they "reap great profit and Advantages to themselves thereby".[11]

The appointment of Robert Byng as governor of Barbados that same year with instructions to do all in his power to secure the "peaceable explusion" of the French from the islands in question, served to heighten the tension already surrounding the issue.[12] It was soon evident that the French had no intention of honoring the terms of the twenty-five year old treaty, and that no steps short of military force could expel them from their footholds on the several islands.

In one of Byng's first communications to the Board he acknowledged the "great Prejudice which arises to Our Sugar Colonies by the secret Introduction of French Sugars into them and the particular injury it is to this island . . .".[13] In a postscript to the same letter Byng stated that he was trying to remove the French from St. Lucia and St. Vincent, but was pessimistic about the success of his efforts.[14]

The sad plight of the Barbados planters bears adequate testimony to the inroads made by the French in their successful usurpation of the colonial sugar market. The extent of the French penetration into the British sugar market was all the more remarkable since it continued to increase in spite of legislation designed to halt its spread. In June 1739, after years of effort, Parliament gave its approval, with restrictions, to a plan to allow the direct exportation of British sugar to the European market.

The Sugar Act, as it was called, permitted the British planters to ship sugar directly to any European port, and removed all the import and re-export duties formerly collected in Britain. The only restrictions placed upon this trade were that ships sailing to ports north of Cape Finisterre touch at some British port,[15] and that only ships built and

[10] *Idem.*
[11] Dottin to Board of Trade, 28 May 1739. *C.O.* 28:25, Aa. 76.
[12] Byng was appointed, 31 May 1739. *C.O.* 28:25, Aa. 74, 75.
[13] Byng to Board of Trade, 7 January 1740. *C.O.* 28:25, Aa. 80.
[14] *Idem.*
[15] Cape Finistere in Spain.

TABLE II

Average Price per Hundredweight of Barbados Muscovado Sugar Sold at the London Custom House, 1750-1787

	Bottom	Average	Top
1750		27s. 9½d.	
1751		30s. 6d.	
1752		38s. 7¼d.	
1753		33s.	
1754		35s. 8¾d.	
1755		35s. 8¾d.	
1756		34s. 3¼d.	
1757		37s. 1d.	
1758		42s. 5¼d.	
1759		45s. 9d.	
1760	32s.	39s. 7¾d.	47s.
1761	32s.	36s. 4d.	50s.
1762	28s.	40s. 8d.	49s.
1763	25s.	32s. 6d.	37s.
1764	27s.	30s. 9d.	40s.
1765	32s.	38s. 1d.	44s.
1766	29s.	38s. 3¼d.	42s.
1767	33s.	35s. 11d.	42s.
1768	32s.	34s. 8d.	41s.
1769	33s.	37s. 2½d.	42s.
1770	31s.	36s.	42s.
1771	32s.	36s. 10¾d.	44s.
1772	29s.	36s.	43s.
1773	28s.	36s. 6d.	45s.
1774	27s.	missing	44s.
1775	25s.	missing	39s.
1776	29s.	37s. 2½d.	47s.
1777	39s.	51s. 8½d.	65s.
1778	45s.	51s. 4¼d.	68s.
1779	50s.		59s.
1780	45s.		59s.
1781	56s.		73s.
1782	40s.		73s.
1783	28s.		45s.
1784	26s.		46s.
1785	35s.		45s.
1786	40s.		56s.
1787	41s.		52s.

Edwards, *op. cit.*, II, p. 267; Add. M. 8133c ff. 224-226.

owned in Britain engage in the trade.[16] The act gave notice to France and the mainland colonists that Parliament had become concerned for the welfare of the sugar islands, even at the expense of other parts of the British empire.

Sugar prices on the London market reacted swiftly to the passage of the act by staging an immediate rise,[17] but to credit the Sugar Act alone for this sudden prosperity would be erroneous indeed. Muscovado rose from an average of 21s. 7¾d. per hundredweight in 1738, to 25s. 8¼d. in 1739, and to 32s. ½d. in 1740,[18] partially because the planters no longer needed to ship the bulk of their produce to England to be sold at whatever price was offered, but primarily because of the renewal of formal sea warfare between Britain and Spain in the Caribbean in 1739.

War, or the threat of it, always caused a general price rise in sugar and other West Indian products in Britain, as the general cost of shipping and insurance increased tremendously during wartime, especially when the sea lanes between Europe and the Caribbean were endangered. Thus the difficulty in attributing the immediate rise in the price of sugar to the Act of 1739 lies in the fact that the 1740's were years of war in which, ultimately, the French colonies became involved. Still, the average price of muscovado during the six years of peace between 1749 and 1755 was 31s. 1¼d., and the lowest only 27s. 9½d.[19]

This certainly suggests that the greatest advantage of the act lay in the better bargaining position that it gave to the planters in their dealings with the London sugar dealers for very little trade with Europe actually resulted from its passage. The restrictions imposed by the act were such that only forty-eight licenses were granted to ship sugar from the West Indies directly to points in Europe south of Cape Finisterre between 1739 and 1753, and of these only five were ever used.[20] It was the possibility of sending sugar directly to the continent, rather than the deed, and the increasing effectiveness of

[16] In 1742 the privilege was extended to colonial ships at the request of the Barbadians who claimed they were suffering for lack of British shipping due to the war. It is a tribute to the increased political strength of the planters that this change could be accomplished in the face of strong opposition from British shipping interests.

[17] See Table II.

[18] See Table II.

[19] See Table II.

[20] Pitman, *op. cit.*, p. 184.

the West Indian planter groups in London, that raised its price on the British sugar market and circumvented any possible price collusion by a refiners association.[21]

The outbreak of fighting with Spain in 1739 and the improvement in the price of sugar did not get at the basic difficulty facing the Barbadians and indeed all the British planters. This was the distortion of trade caused by the efficient French and abetted by the price conscious British colonists from North America. The war with Spain barely caused a ripple of excitement on the mainland outside of Georgia and South Carolina. Actually, prospects of an easier and more open trade with the French islands appeared enhanced with the British navy now sailing in search of the Spaniard rather than colonial interlopers.

Until the renewal of fighting against France in 1742, the three years of improved sugar prices occasioned by the Spanish War meant little material gain for the Barbadians. Increases in shipping and insurance charges on homeward cargoes accounted for most of the rise in price, and a similar jump in the cost of provisions destined for the British islands leaves some doubt as to whether or not the planters were able to share in the blessings of the price rise.

The advantages of a Spanish war were not altogether lost on the Barbadians however, and those planters who had been active in urging a British penetration of the "neutral islands" now encouraged the taking of Trinidad for the purpose of increasing British sugar production, and for its settlement opportunities. Governor Byng was a strong advocate of the scheme, and viewed the proposal as a means of relieving most of the planter distress caused by the poor soil of Barbados. He was quick to urge the capture of Trinidad and felt that it could be done with ease as it was reported to have a garrison of only three hundred Spanish troops.[22] Unfortunately from their point of view the outbreak of war with France spelled an end to the hope of a Barbadian migration to the fresh soil of Trinidad.[23]

[21] Makinson, *op. cit.*, p. 132.

[22] Byng to Board of Trade, 23 June 1740. *C.O.* 28:25, Aa. 89.

[23] The War with Spain beginning in 1739 grew out of commercial rivalry between the two powers and was but a prelude to the larger war of the Austrian Succession three years later. The Spanish-British conflict is usually referred to as the War of Jenkins Ear, taking its name from an incident in 1731 when Robert Jenkins, captain of an English merchant vessel, claimed to have had his ear cut off by an officer of a Spanish guarda costa in retaliation for smuggling with Cuba. Continued British smuggling activity and resentment at exclusion from the

That same year Byng's attempt to strike more effectively at the constant violations of the Acts of Trade by colonial ships was dealt a heavy blow by the Board of Trade. Following the start of hostilities in 1739, Byng gave his assent to the seizing of colonial and neutral shipping in the harbors of Barbados that was found to be carrying cargo prohibited by the Navigation Acts. The owners of several ships thus seized appealed to the Board for redress of this "arbitrary" action by Byng and his naval commanders, on the grounds that unless such goods were actually confiscated by customs while being smuggled ashore, they were not in violation of the law. The mere possession of such goods on board ship, they felt, should not be considered prima-facie evidence of smuggling.

The Governor also wrote to the Board stating his views on the seizures, and attempted to justify his action by citing the harmful effects of such underhanded trade on the Barbados economy. The Board sought a ruling on the legality of the in-port seizures from the Solicitor-General, and upon his recommendation ruled the seizures illegal.[24]

This was a serious setback for the zealous Governor Byng, and a blow to those who had profited from the sale of seized merchandise. It was however, a fortunate decision for the vast majority of Barbadians, for news of Byng's action had swept the length of the Caribbean and many ships carrying needed provisions from the northern colonies had ceased to call at Barbados for fear of forcible confiscation of all or part of their cargoes. With the threat of a new French conflict daily growing stronger, the Barbadians sought to stockpile sufficient food and material for their use in case of isolation or attack, but the decrease in the number of supply ships arriving in their harbors made this an impossible undertaking. It was not until news of the Board's decision reached the Indies in late 1740 that North American shipping once again arrived in adequate numbers to allow the storage of supplies on the island.

In 1741 word was received on Barbados of a bill then in Parliament that would prohibit the export of corn (wheat) and other provisions from Great Britain, Ireland, and His Majesty's possessions in North

---

Spanish colonial trade caused the war, but Jenkins' story in the House of Commons, complete with the holding aloft of his severed ear, made a tremendous impact on British national pride and eventually forced the reluctant Sir Robert Walpole to declare war.

[24] Frances Fane to Board of Trade, 15 August 1740. *C.O.* 28:25, Aa. 93.

America for the duration of the war then about to begin in Europe. The news created an immediate wave of hysteria throughout the island and food prices rose drastically on the assumption that the bill, if passed, would create a further shortage of provisions than that normally experienced and expected during wartime.[25] The Assembly immediately sent a protest to the Board against any action that would create further hardship for the island and her sister colonies in the West Indies.[26]

While promotion of such an act was clearly designed to hamper the internal economies of Britain's continental enemies and, if effective in its sanctions, would be likely to create a surplus of export grain and thus tend to lower prices and benefit the West Indian buyer, this knowledge seems to have escaped the planters. Gripped by their fear of abandonment by the mother country because their isolated position might be difficult to defend in wartime, the planters continued to be irrational and shortsighted in much of their outlook toward empire affairs. Laws prohibiting the export of provisions of any kind from Barbados had been passed fifty years before and still remained in force as testimony to the always-present fear of shortage. Merchants desiring to export livestock or provisions needed permission from the Governor and his Council even in times of peace.[27]

Throughout 1740 and 1741 the West Indies reflected the steadily worsening situation in Europe. Shortly before his sudden death in October 1740, Byng reported failure in his efforts to secure the peaceable removal of the French garrisons from St. Lucia, and St. Vincent. In reply to his letter to the French urging them to honor their treaty obligations, the Governor of Martinique announced French claim to St. Lucia by right of first settlement, and stated that St. Vincent and Dominica belonged to the Caribs.[28] Since the Caribs were unwilling hosts to large groups of French settlers on all three islands, this was tantamount to proclaming de jure as well as de facto settlement by the French.

The loyal President of Council, James Dottin, was required to assume executive leadership of Barbados once again upon the death

[25] 11 June 1741. *C.O.* 31:21. Many of the volumes in this series are neither lettered nor numbered by folio or page; thus the seemingly inadequate designation by volume only must be used.

[26] *Idem.*

[27] Permission to export was often granted in peacetime after the payment of a £25 fee to have a permission petition read before the Governor-in-Council.

[28] Byng to Board of Trade, 13 August 1740. *C.O.* 28:25, Aa. 94.

of Byng, and he immediately began efforts to strengthen the island's defenses and waken the Assembly members to a sense of their responsibility toward the safety of the colony. Dottin championed the Assembly's view on changing the $4\frac{1}{2}$ percent, however, and used the threat of war and possible French attack to urge the use of the export tax funds for defense purposes.[29] In a petition to the king in 1741 the Assembly stressed the inability of the planters to assume any additional burdens of taxation, and enclosed an accounting of the expenditures from the $4\frac{1}{2}$ percent through February 1741, as proof of its misuse.[30]

Barbados had in fact become so impoverished that the Assembly was forced to pass new legislation aimed at preventing the flight of debtors from the island.[31] Action of this nature in addition to a renewal of petitioning for economic and tax relief bear adequate testimony to the ineffectiveness of the Molasses and Sugar Acts of the previous decade. These acts designed to mitigate the financial stress of the British colonies, and the older island in particular, had failed to achieve their purpose because of widespread evasion and improper enforcement. But even if the acts had been effective in archieving their stated purposes, they were not a remedy for the chief economic ills of the older islands – loss of productivity and high duties on export commodities.

The threat of an enlarged war added to the uneasiness already gripping the West Indies. Reports of renewed French activity on the neutral islands and a strenghtening of their military establishment on Martinique were forwarded to Whitehall from Dottin and the other British colonial executives.[32] The planters while encouraged by the upward trend of London sugar prices, were vexed by higher prices for their own needs, and the uncertainty of their future in the face of a prolonged French war.

Planter pessimism was heightened by the steady flow of French products going northword in the holds of colonial ships, much of it paid for with hard money taken in exchange for needed provisions

[29] *C.O.* 28:25, Aa. 105. The request was not granted. See 8 October 1741. *C.O.* 31:21.

[30] *C.O.* 28:25, Aa. 104. The date 5 February 1740, on the document would correspond with the year 1741 by present day Gregorian calculations. It was not until 1752 that the British Julian calendar was modified to conform with the continental and presently accepted calendar.

[31] *C.O.* 28:25, Aa. 106.

[32] Dottin to Board of Trade, 22 October 1740, 16 July 1741. *C.O.* 28:25, Aa. 100; *C.O.* 28:25, Aa. 107.

from the Barbadians themselves. Many of the northern captains, who formerly stopped at Barbados, were now making St. Lucia a port of call instead, and as the size and productivity of the French colony increased the volume of mainland shipping rose accordingly. The planter dominated Assembly constantly harassed Governor Byng and President Dottin to take a more positive type of action against the French than the mere sending of notes to rid Barbados of that "great discouragement of trade" one hundred miles to the Northwest.[33] The Assembly noted that French sugar, rum, and molasses continued to pour into the northern colonies at lower cost than British produce in spite of the Molasses Act, thus creating a need for more stringent measures to control foreign competition.[34]

The wheels of government turn slowly; government circles were aware of the failure of the Acts of 1733 and 1739 to correct a difficult situation, but relief in the form of proper enforcement of the existing laws or new legislation was not forthcoming for another two decades. We may offer the outbreak of war in 1739 as an excuse for the government's failure to take concerted action in an area so vital to the welfare of an important segment of its empire, but we may also ask whether the renewal of the bitter struggle with France would not make such action almost imperative for the safety of those British islands in the West Indies upon which so much depended. The islands were at once an area of production of important tropical commodities bartered by British merchants throughout the world, a market for British manufactures second only to the thirteen northern colonies within the empire, a source of Anglo influence in the Hispanic American empire, and strategic centers of British military and naval forces in the New World.

The British West Indies deserved a better fate than to languish for fifty years while fellow colonists were able to reap fat profits from an identical trade carried on with others. While much of the planters' misery was of their own making through wastefulness and greed, a more knowledgeable course of colonial administration on the part of Whitehall could have overcome much the distress engendered in the Caribbean by this lack of direction from above. The sugar islands had been placed in a position of restraint not unlike that which gradually enveloped the northern colonies after 1764. For the colonists on the mainland there were avenues of evasion and the means at hand to

[33] Minutes of the Assembly, 10 January 1740. *C.O.* 31:22.
[34] *Idem.*

exert counterpressures on the mother country, plus a land richly endowed in raw materials for a good start in the direction of self-sufficiency; for the West Indians there was little recourse but to submit. The Acts were often evaded, and many times evasion of the trade laws meant the difference between profit and loss, survival or not surviving, but evasion was only a prevention of harm, not a cure for the disease that slowly ate away the vitality of the sugar colonies. Outposts surrrounded by hostile neighbors and dependent upon a tenuous line of supply for their very existence could not exhibit the daring of their continental brethren in voting retaliatory measures against the crown.

The islands entered the middle stage of the Anglo-French conflict without hope that either victory or defeat would alter their situation in the least.

By 1741 the Caribbean swarmed with privateers, and shipping costs rose to cover the increased danger of capture or destruction. On Barbados the presence of these ships was acutely felt in the higher prices of most commodities and services. Despairing of receiving help in the form of a warship from the Admiralty, the merchants and planters determined to secure the necessary funds for the equipping of a ship of their own to keep the island's coastal waters free from danger. The movement commenced soon after the start of the Spanish War; one year later the project had still not met with success.[35] In December 1741, the Council petitioned the king for a naval squadron to protect Barbados from the French in case of war and from the current depredations of privateers on the island's shipping,[36] and as late as June 1743, the merchants petitioned the Board of Trade for protection from Spanish privateers.[37] It is not known whether or not the Barbadians succeeded in their effort at self-defense, for early in 1744 full-scale naval warfare erupted between Britain and France in the West Indies.

During wartime the possibility of invasion always loomed large in

[35] On 8 July 1740 the Assembly reported to Governor Byng that they were still trying to get a ship equipped for action against the privateers. *C.O.* 31:22.

[36] Petition to George II from the Barbados Council, 11 December 1741. *C.O.* 31:21.

[37] The merchants of Barbados to Board of Trade, 25 June 1743. *C.O.* 28:46, no. 37. Another memorial was sent to the Governor by the merchants on 16 March 1743, complaining of losses occasioned by Spanish and *French* privateers. It is interesting to note that this was a year before notification of war between Britain and France was received from London marking the official start of hostilities. *C.O.* 31:21; *C.O.* 28:46, no. 76.

the thoughts of the island residents, and defense policy was directed solely toward repelling invasion attempts. Offensive action against the enemy could never be considered by island militia groups, and the active prosecution of a war had to be left in the hands of the Royal Navy and the regular military establishment. Militia units often partook in joint efforts with the regulars (often to the consternation of both groups), but operations which involved the transportation of large numbers of men and supplies across many miles of rough sea had to be, of necessity, the prerogative of a professional military organization.

With little possibility for offensive action at hand, the war years became primarily a time of semi-isolation and suspense. Trade was apt to slow down compared with peacetime, but it did not, and could not, cease altogether. In matters of trade the British islands were always better off than their French neighbors thanks to the protection of the usually superior and more numerous British fleet, and beginning in 1744 two large convoys sailed each year between England and Barbados bringing provisions and carrying away sugar products.[38]

The war years appear to have brought only subtle changes to the colony. In spite of the war, privateering, and the presence of large portions of the British, French, and Spanish navies in adjacent waters, a sizeable trade continued to take place in the Antilles and with the British colonists in North America.[39] The unique and interesting facet of the wartime trade was that carried on between the combatants, often in an open fashion at the height of the fighting.

Although illicit trade had assumed considerable proportions in the commerce of the Caribbean for at least three decades, the casual observer might expect the passions of war to stifle it quickly enough. Such was not the case in the ten years of conflict after 1739. The new Governor of Barbados, Thomas Robinson, was beset by a continuous traffic in provisions and sugar between that island and the French islands, particularly the bastion of Martinique one hundred twenty miles to the Northwest.

The French planters on Martinique hard pressed to market all of their huge crop with the eager North Americans, turned increasingly to the device of disposing part of their surplus in the British islands. On Barbados, local merchants able to buy high-quality French sugars at moderate prices from the French captains who called at the island,

[38] *C.O.* 31:25.

[39] See the Barbados shipping returns for 1747 in Table III. *C.O.* 33:16.

TABLE III

Barbados Shipping Returns, 1747
Number of Ships Entering and Leaving

From:		To:	
Philadelphia	21	Philadelphia	24
Virginia	19	Virginia	21
London	14	London	16
Connecticut	9	Newfoundland	9
South Carolina	6	Liverpool	7
Newfoundland	5	Connecticut	7
Salem	5	Cork	7
Africa	4	Salem	6
Maine	4	Antigua	6
Esquebo	4	South Carolina	6
Belfast	3	Esquebo	4
Dublin	3	Falmouth	3
Marblehead	3	Maine	3
Madeira	3	Maryland	3
Antigua	3	St. Kitts	3
Cork	3	Bermuda	3
Liverpool	2	Bristol	3
Delaware	2	Surinam	2
New York	2	Isle of Man	2
St. Eustatius	1	Marblehead	2
Falmouth	1	Belfast	2
Gurnsey	1	Rhode Island	2
Lisbon	1	Aquilla	2
Cape Verde Island	1	Dublin	2
Rhode Island	1	New York	2
North Carolina	1	Turks and Cocos Is.	2
Anguilla	1	Curacao	2
Newburyport	1	Jamaica	2
Glasgow	1	Boston	1
Maryland	1	Newburyport	1
Boston	1	St. Eustatius	1
		Plymouth	1

C.O. 33:16, part 2.

introduced their purchases into the regular channels as locally produced, and marketed most of it at premium prices on the London market. This particular trade was especially hard on the planters already beset by numerous difficulties in the marketing of their sugars, and Governor Robinson was diligent in his efforts to put an end to it. He became increasingly irritated at his own customs officials as he became aware of their complicity in these smuggling activities, and waged a ceaseless war of words against them and their deeds for the remainder of his term of office. But the Governor was powerless to act in the face of determined opposition from most of the merchants and many of the planters. For the French trade, harmful as it might be, was still a source of profit to many men of influence on the island, and without their active support the Governor could do little.

In addition to their sugar sales on Barbados the French soon became important buyers of slaves. During most of the 1740's they made steady purchases of excess Negroes from planters who, owing to the war, found themselves oversupplied and from slave merchants whose route to Africa was protected by the Royal Navy and could always guarantee an ample supply.[40] The fact that many of the slaves were shipped to St. Lucia to aid in the French settlement of that island was all the more painful to Governor Robinson.[41] The slave purchases from the British were but a fraction of the total, and the expansion of the production potential of the French colonies in the years to come was to create a more serious threat to British welfare than any military prowess possessed by the French.[42]

The documents of the period are filled with references to this illegal trade, and Governor Robinson's futile efforts to correct the situation. There was so little need for secrecy and so little danger of official action against them, that the French traders felt free to move about the harbor and town of Bridgetown at will. One such pair of French merchants was accosted by the Governor as they strolled openly through the marketplace of the capital, and to the astonishment of both parties they were not arrested on the spot. The Governor could only threaten them with imprisonment unless they left the island within *twenty four hours*![43]

Governor Robinson, badly shaken by his lack of effectiveness in dealing with this wholesale violation of the law on the part of his citizens, could only offer excuses to his superiors and promises of more effort on his part. He was not wholly to blame, for illicit trade between Barbados and Martinique had been "carried on for some

[40] Robinson to Board of Trade, 27 November 1742. *C.O.* 28:26, Bb. 1. For direct quote see Chapter I, page 16.

[41] *Idem.*

[42] In 1742 a British captain who had brought 123 Negroes to Barbados from the Gold Coast reported that he had seen forty French ships there engaged in purchasing slaves for delivery to the French West Indies. *C.O.* 28:46, no. 2.

[43] It is safe to assume that the unpopular Robinson was powerless to make an arrest and could only shout abuses and threats at the surprised Frenchmen. Robinson to Council, 2 November 1742. *C.O.* 31:21.

years past . . .",[44] and the Governor was "powerless" to act alone. Robinson was also aware of the precarious position of Barbados during wartime and the inability of her soil to support her large population. With the rumor of a French invasion at hand, Robinson was forced to admit that the island was suffering for lack of supplies and could not expect to withstand a prolonged seige.[45] We can only surmise to what extent French provisions illegally procured may have saved Barbados from mass starvation and the complete ruin of her economy.

To combat the threat to his island's shipping the Governor began to license privateers on his own authority soon after his arrival on the island. For the payment of a £25 fee the master of any ship trading to Barbados could secure authorization to engage in the ancient art of privateering. We are led to believe that the Governor's motive was less that of granting protection and revenge for the sea captains and shipowners, than that of an interest in obtaining the £25 per document, for the privilege was soon abused by most of those holding licenses. Word quickly reached the Admiralty and the Board of Trade of numerous captures of Dutch and Danish vessels on the pretext of their carrying Spanish goods.

Since the Governor had no authorization to license privateers in his instructions, and little, if any, precedent for such action existed without previous approval from the home government, Robinson was finally ordered to cease the practice on the grounds that his actions were endangering the good relations between Great Britain and the Netherlands.[46]

The already strained financial condition of Barbados was made considerably worse by the additional burden of war. The expense of maintainng an enlarged garrison of regular troops, combined with a drop in tax revenues owing to a decrease in the volume of regular trade increased the Assembly's already strong opposition toward the needless allocation of funds.

Because of the Barbadians' unwillingness to do more on their own behalf the protection of the island remained the prerogative of the military and naval commanders in the area, and their superiors in London. The crown was also hard pressed financially to fight a war

[44] Robinson to Duke of Newcastle, 22 April 1743. *C.O.* 28:46, no. 21.
[45] Robinson to Duke of Newcastle, 23 April 1745. *C.O.* 28:46, no. 129.
[46] The Court of St. James, 13 April 1743. Warrant issued to Governor Robinson to observe the Treaty of 1674 between Great Britain and Holland. *C.O.* 28:41.

on many fronts throughout the world and soon determined to take matters in hand by raising additional tax monies wherever possible. In the spring of 1744 Parliament debated levying a 2s. 4d. tax increase on all imported sugar as a means of securing additional funds. News of the bill set off a flurry of protest from the planting interest throughout the islands. Instances of the declining state of the various colonies were recounted in great detail, outlining once again the value of the islands to the crown and the various commercial interests of the mother country.

Since the Barbadians had already protested the old tax rates on sugar in previous memorials, the new rates coming on top of the 4½ percent duty were looked upon with considerable abhorrence.[47] Robinson was quick to call the attention of the Board to the plight of his island already "weighted down" by the burden of heavy taxation and poor soil.[48] He also noted that many planters were moving to Dutch settlements where taxes were lower and the soil newer and more fertile.[49] The Dutch colony at the mouth of the Esequebo River on the South American mainland had attracted numerous British planters for over a decade, as had the other Dutch settlements along the Orinoco and Demerara Rivers nearby. Through the years of low sugar prices in the 1720's a steady trickle of British island planters flowed southward to escape their financial fate and commence anew their pattern of life amid more favorable circumstances in the Dutch colonies.

Robinson and his associates on the other islands were acutely aware of this steady drain on their dominions and its probable consequences for the safety of the empire in the West Indies if allowed to go unchallenged. The Barbadians favored an increase in the tax on rum in lieu of a general raise on all sugars. Since very little rum was exported in proportion to sugar and molasses, this would be less of a hardship than any other type of an increase levied on exports. Quoting the results of a 4½d. increase in rates effected on Jamaican rum a few years before, Robinson boosted a rum tax as the most equitable method for raising additional funds.[50]

[47] Petition of the Barbados Council and Assembly, 23 November 1743. *C.O.* 31:23.

[48] Robinson to Board of Trade, 10 May 1744. *C.O.* 28:26, Bb. 11.

[49] *Idem.*

[50] *Ibid.*, 29 April 1746. *C.O.* 31:23. Jamaica supposedly raised £43,565 via the new tax in five years.

The tax threat evaporated when the wretched condition of the British colonies precluded any immediate action by Parliament hard pressed by more urgent matters of war.[51] As the struggle progressed to a conclusion in Europe and North America, Barbados suffered no worse fate than one invasion scare in 1745 and the hardship of a disruption of her normal trade channels for six years.[52] These events were disturbing enough however in light of other French successes in the Antilles. Early in the war St. Lucia was occupied by a strong force of six hundred regular French troops, thus shattering the flimsy pretense of neutrality for that island,[53] and in 1748 a strong force of French regulars and militia from Martinique occupied Tobago without a struggle.[54] It was quite obvious that the trade war was not being won by force of arms, and that recent French successes in occupying fertile islands, if not undone at the peace conference, promised continued French competition from a position of strength unequaled in the one hundred year old commercial rivalry.

The taking of Tobago was especially bothersome to the Barbadians, because of its closeness to Barbados and its proximity to Trinidad still weakly held by a small number of Spanish settlers. The Treaty of Aix-la-Chapelle ordered the return of Tobago, St. Lucia, St. Vincent, and Dominica to the Caribs and the immediate evacuation of all European settlements on the islands. This was, in fact, a return to status quo ante bellum and the re-establishment of the neutral islands.[55]

In principle, the neutralization of islands having conflicting ownership claims against them was sound; in practice the policy resulted in a further deterioration of British-French relations and the eventual

[51] *C.O.* 31:23, page 107.

[52] Robinson to Board of Trade, 23 April 1745. He reported that the invasion fleet contained 482 guns and 4,870 troops. *C.O.* 28:26, Bb. 27. In 1746 Barbados merchants raised £500 to pay far an armed ship to cruise around the island for a week to keep French privateers away. *C.O.* 31:24, no. 36.

[53] Board of Trade to the Duke of Newcastle, 10 October 1744. *C.O.* 28:41, no. 39; Robinson to the Board of Trade, 15 July 1744. *C.O.* 28:26, Bb. 13.

[54] Board of Trade to the Duke of Bedford, 7 December 1748. *C.O.* 28:41, no. 23; Lord Grenville to the Board of Trade, 4 April 1749. *C.O.* 28:41, no. 38: *Ibid.*, 17 October 1748. *C.O.* 28:29, Cc. 15; Committee of Correspondence of Barbados to Agent John Sharp in London, 25 January 1748. Manuscript Room of the British Museum, Additional Manuscript (hereafter cited as Add. M.) 23718, f. 43.

[55] The French claim to Grenada was honored officially, and that island ceased to be neutral after 1748. The British did not press their claim to any of the former neutral islands or Tobago. *C.O.* 28:29, Cc. 17.

founding of French settlements on most. Nine years of intermittent war in the Caribbean had failed to solve the basic antagonisms between the two great powers, and just as in Europe, India, and North America the problems of expansion would again lead to a renewal of the military conflict, so they would also in the West Indies.

III

THE SEVEN YEARS' WAR

The years of peace between 1749 and 1755 were probably the best the Barbados planters had seen for a century. Although sugar prices weakened with the conclusion of the war, this was offset by a drop in freightage and insurance charges on Atlantic shipping. Even during the good years, however, the profits of sugar growing were not extravagant, considering the risks involved. The net profit from a well-managed plantation seldom was more than seven to ten percent even in the best years with ideal growing and marketing conditions, and there were many years when all or part of the sugar crop was lost to the extremities of weather alone.[1] What is remarkable is that the Barbadians were able to maintain such a rate of profit in view of the great production increase which occurred on all of the islands during the first half of the eighteenth century. Both British sugar production and the export of sugar to Great Britain trebled between 1700 and 1760.[2] British importation of empire sugar rose from less than 500,000 hundredweights at the beginning of the century to three times that amount sixty years later.[3] It must be noted that the chief beneficiary of better prices was Jamaica with its vast areas of newly cultivated land; the economy of Barbados and the older sugar islands was merely supported rather than rehabilitated by the continuance of a favorable market.[4]

In answer to a query sent by the Board of Trade, Governor Robinson

[1] W. L. Burn, *The British West Indies* (London, 1951), p. 71.

[2] J. H. Parry and P. M. Sherlock, *A Short History of the West Indies* (London, 1957), p. 117.

[3] Burn, *op. cit.*, p. 71. In using these figures it must be kept in mind that an unknown quantity of French, Dutch, Danish, and Spanish sugar was continually imported into the mother country in the guise of British grown sugar, especially after 1740. For a fuller discussion of this problem and British efforts to combat it see Makinson, *op. cit.*, Chapter Six.

[4] *Idem., Ibid.*, p. 133. Also see Table II, p. 34.

noted the precariousness of Barbados trade even in good times when he acknowledged that the French on St. Lucia were underselling the Barbadians at St. Eustatius, thus hindering "the consumption of our Sugar and Rum in the Northern Colonys . . ., (notably) New England and Rhode Island where the Act of Parliament origin'd for the benefit of the Sugar Colonies has had no effect . . ."[5]

Of more potential danger was the continued French occupation of Tobago in violation of the peace treaty provision for its immediate evacuation. While most of the island was thinly occupied and the main French settlement consisted of little more than "miserable sheds without sides" which functioned as houses, it served to remind the British, and the neighboring Barbadians in particular, of the agressiveness of the French king.[6] Tobago fully planted to sugar could easily outproduce Barbados – perhaps even Antigua and Monteserrat, and in the event of war it would serve to outflank Barbados from still another direction.

It is easy to see why concern ran deep among responsible officials in Britain and in the islands. As early as 1749 conditions were already brewing that would ultimately lead to a renewal of the conflict on a worldwide basis, and it was easy to see that the loss of one island, one fort, or the goodwill of a possible future ally might spell the difference between victory or disaster at some uncertain time in the not too distant future.

Governor Grenville of Barbados faced with the responsibility of forcing the French evacuation of the neutral islands in the Leewards, promoted the idea of an attack on Tobago before the French could fortify the island.[7] He reasoned that a successful attack on one island would give weight to British demands for the evacuation of all. His proposal bears testimony to the seriousness with which the Barbadians viewed the French seizures and their desire for a speedy remedy at any cost.

[5] Robinson to Board of Trade, 20 February 1747. *C.O.* 28:27, Bb. 57. The small Dutch island of St. Eustatius, lying only ten miles from the larger British owned St. Kitts, had long been a free-trade entrepot for merchants of all nations. The Barbadians often disposed of large quantities of sugar in this fashion, particularly if the London price was sluggish, or wartime conditions endangered or limited homeward voyages.

[6] Report of Captain Thomas Sayer to Governor Thomas Grenville of Barbados, 20 November 1748. *C.O.* 28:29, Cc. 21. Captain Sayer had scouted Tobago on instructions from Governor Grenville, who hoped to evict the French forcibly if they were not too strongly garrisoned.

[7] Grenville to Board of Trade, 12 December 1748. *C.O.* 28:29, Cc. 18.

The home government preferred to bring about the evacuation of Tobago and the other neutral islands by negotiation rather than force of arms, and entrusted Governor Grenville with the responsibility of carrying out those aims. Late in 1749 Grenville reached agreement with the Marquis de Caylus, Governor of Martinique for a common evacuation of Tobago, and on the strength of it published the proclamation on Barbados.[8] In February 1750, Grenville proclaimed the evacuation of all four islands. He assured the cooperation of the Caylus, or perhaps by this time wished to prod him into action, for the French remained noticeably sluggish in their efforts to comply with the agreement – a position which was to characterize their actions during the seven years of peace prior to 1756.[9]

Only a month later Grenville was forced to report to the Board of Trade that de Caylus had refused to act until he was officially instructed to do so by his king. When the Martinique governor was reminded that the French king had signed the articles of peace providing for the evacuations, he remained adamant.[10] Still Grenville was optimistic of eventual success with the French and wrote encouragingly of his efforts in his reports home during the early months of negotiations.[11]

The Barbados governor resolved to be patient in the face of an increasing number of reports of French vacillation. Commodore Holborn, the senior naval officer, reported the he personally doubted that the French intended to evacuate St. Lucia and Dominica, those islands "being well settled, and looked upon as their own" by those in authority.[12] Negotiations were further complicated by British gunners on Nevis who had mistakenly fired on a French ship, thus giving the French a legitimate talking point in the face of British demands for cooperation.[13]

Governor de Caylus died unexpectedly in May 1750, thus causing an additional delay in the negotiations until a successor could be

[8] The agreement was signed on Martinique, 27 November 1749. *C.O.* 28:29, Cc. 44; *C.O.* 28:29, Cc. 46.

[9] 20 February 1740. *C.O.* 28:29, Cc. 55.

[10] Grenville to Board of Trade, 13 March 1750. *C.O.* 28:29, Cc. 52.

[11] *Idem.*

[12] Commodore Holborn to Governor Grenville, 11 March 1750. *C.O.* 28:29, Cc. 58.

[13] Grenville to Board of Trade, 20 April 1750. Because of the incident Commodore Holborn was poorly received by French officials on Martinique when he went there with messages from Governor Grenville. *C.O.* 28:29, Cc. 74.

appointed.[14] The new Governor resolved to play the game of frustration with greater skill than his predecessor, and in this respect was remarkably successful. In his first official act Governor Bompar announced that the French could evacuate only St. Lucia.[15] Then he abruptly proclaimed the evacuation of all the islands in question early in 1751.[16] By May the British had begun to realize the cunning of their opponent when it became clear that in spite of the proclamations the French were still firmly entrenched on the four islands and actually increasing their strength and the size of their settlements![17]

By 1752 it had become obvious that nothing short of an armed attack would dislodge the French from their positions on the four islands. Repeated reminders and warnings from the British were usually acknowledged and ignored by French officials;[18] by 1755 the reminders had become protests and the warnings more severe in their tone.[19] With the approach of a new war the flow of communications ceased altogether.

While government officials busied themselves with diplomatic messages on the "neutral islands" affair, the planters of Barbados began to feel and react increasing sugar competition from the four French acquisitions. The detrimental effect of a flood of additional high quality produce on free-market sugar prices can be detected before the close of the War of Austrian Succession. Governor Robinson acknowledged that the French from St. Lucia were underselling the Barbadians as early as 1747,[20] and memorials and petitions on the French danger began to appear with the cessation of hostilities a year later.[21]

[14] Grenville to Board of Trade, 25 May 1750. *C.O.* 28:29, Cc. 83; *Ibid.*, 20 October 1750. *C.O.* 28:29, Cc. 98.

[15] Grenville to Board of Trade, 11 November 1750. *C.O.* 28:29, Cc. 99.

[16] 15 January 1751. *C.O.* 28:29, Cc. 111.

[17] Grenville to Board of Trade, 25 May 1751. *C.O.* 28:29, Cc. 121.

[18] Grenville to Board of Trade, 4 August 1752. *C.O.* 28:30, Dd. 4.;*Ibid.*, 14 December 1752. *C.O.* 28:30, Dd. 20.

[19] President Ralph Weeks to Board of Trade, 24 September 1755. *C.O.* 28:30, Dd. 83, 85, 86.

[20] See footnote 5 above.

[21] Memorial of Dominic Lynch to Board of Trade, 2 May 1748. *C.O.* 28:29, Cc. 2. Lynch claimed that "the French have settled in force during the present war [and] this will obstruct navigation and injure the sugar trade".; Grenville to Board of Trade, 3 April 1749. *C.O.* 28:29, Cc. 28. He stated that the French were strong, "and are very numerous". Petition of Council and Assembly of Barbados to George II, 15 December 1749. *C.O.* 31:25. Petitioners stated that the French settlement on Tobago endangered the price of Barbados sugar and the safety of the island.

The seriousness of the situation was complicated by the acknowledged failure of the Sugar Act and the reluctance of Parliament to take positive remedial measures since its passage in 1739. Grenville stated that under the auspices of the Act "not above three or four vessels were overloaded for the straights and none at all for any foreign port to the Northward of Cape Finisterre".[22] American traders were heavy buyers of French sugars at all times, not having been slowed at all in their accustomed dealings with the French by Parliamentary legislation or their own kinship to fellow countrymen in the West Indies. The Barbados governor remarked on this, stating that the French islands produce sugar in "much greater abundance and much less expense, and they pay lower duties, whereby they can afford to undersell us in every Foreign Market in Europe; they permit and encourage an extensive clandestine trade with all the British Colonies in North America".[23]

Much of the difficulty could be traced directly to planter dependence on sugar as the sole crop throughout most of the West Indies. Old cultivation habits ran deep among the planters and occasional efforts to get some of them to switch to other types of agriculture usually proved futile. In commenting upon an act of Parliament passed in 1748, to encourage the raising of indigo, Grenville remarked that, "of this I can foresee but little Prospect, all the Planters of this Island [are] devoting their whole thoughts entirely to the cultivation of Sugar Canes, even to an exclusion of almost all other commodities".[24]

It was quite obvious that the Barbadians were in the unenviable position of having to rely upon the services of those chiefly responsible for their deteriorating local market position. The Americans continued to be the prime suppliers of provisions, livestock, and building materials for most of the West Indies, while selectively purchasing varying quantities of sugar products from whoever offered the lowest price consistent with quality. The freedom with which the Americans operated in their West Indian trading ventures was, of course, brought about by their constant violation of the Navigation Acts, and the inability or unwillingness of the home government to take some sort of positive action against them.

This lack of constructive remedies or positive leadership from

[22] Grenville to Board of Trade, 3 April 1749. *C.O.* 28:29, Cc. 28.
[23] *Idem.*
[24] *Ibid.*, 17 October 1748. *C.O.* 28:29, Cc. 15.

London can easily be traced to the presence of opposing pressure groups and vested interests in the Commons – none capable of directing policy, but several possessed of sufficient strength to constitute an effective barrier to the passage of needed legislation. This impasse did not deter the West Indians from making their feelings known however, and with the prospect of a further increase in the power of the sugar lobby in the years to come, the planters wasted no time in lambasting their mainland brethern for their commercial sins.

When it became obvious by 1751 that French occupation of the neutral islands would not soon be ended, an increasing barrage of complaints was leveled at the Americans for their trade transactions with foreigners. The success of the French venture depended to a great extent upon their ability to market the additional sugars produced on the new land at a profit. The American traders guaranteed them this market in their eagerness to purchase at the lowest possible price unencumbered by restrictions and regulations; every shipment of French sugar into the northern colonies meant one more lost sale for the British planters.

As they had done for generations the Barbadians, hampered by their additional tax burden of the $4\frac{1}{2}$ percent, assumed the leadership in attacking "the destructive trade carried on between the northern colonies and the foreign sugar settlements".[25] The extent of French inroads on British commerce and the weakness of the Molasses Act in bringing about some equity to the trade picture can be seen from the following address of the Barbados Assembly in 1751: "The French sugars, rum, and molasses imported into Your Majesty's Northern Colonies . . . are most fraudulently concealed under the legal authentication of British registers."[26] Payment was made in specie usually earned by the Americans in the British West Indies, thus creating an acute shortage of hard currency among the British planters and merchants already hard pressed for coinage by the nature of their economic relationship with Great Britain. The address went on to state: "The commodities of their growth [France] are not importable into the French sugar islands, except in the instance of such few commodities as they can supply themselves with from their own Northern Settlements. This trade gluts our own markets, (and our

[25] Barbados Assembly and Council to George II, 14 May 1751. *C.O.* 31:26.
[26] *Ibid.*, 29 October 1751. *C.O.* 31:26.

price is fallen) in proportion as the quantity at market increases without an additioal demand."[27]

The Barbados legislators argued for a remedy based on the time-honored method of strict enforcement of the Navigation Acts, but added an alternative proposal which was to mark the beginning of an expansion of the free trade principle established with the Act of 1739. They proposed to remedy the worsening situation by

> either . . . absolutely prohibiting all foreign imports of sugar, rum, molasses, and parcels into Your Majesty's Northern Colonies in America, and subjecting the vessels laden with such commodities to seizure upon the high seas and confiscation, or if an illicit trade cannot be entirely prevented, or should it be thought that there is a necessity for supplying Your Majesty's Northern Colonies with a larger quantity of sugar, rum, and molasses than your British sugar colonies can furnish them with at reasonable prices; that then a free and open trade be allowed to be carried on in all Your Majesty's colonies with all foreign states under proper regulations and restrictions.[28]

An example of the seriousness with which the Barbadians viewed the illegal usurpation of their sugar trade was the willingness of the Assembly voluntarily to share in the expense of prosecuting offenders before the courts. The otherwise parsimonious legislature was quick to react to a report from the Antigua Assembly complaining of the importation of Danish sugar by Great Britain, and the fraudulent importation of French sugar and rum labeled as British produce.[29] Suspecting dishonest customs officials, both Assemblies agreed to underwrite the cost of bringing them to justice, and halting any trade that "is in any way hurtful to the British Sugar Colonies".[30]

Efforts to redress the economic balance came to a sudden end in 1756 with the renewal of warfare for the fourth time in sixty-five years between the crowns of Great Britain and France. The conflict which was to follow in the next seven years would set the stage for the final drama of partition within the old British empire, while simultaneously achieving for Britain her greatest moment of colonial supremacy.

Despite the magnitude of the Seven Years' War and the ineptitude with which it was waged by the British until 1758, Barbados suffered little at the hands of the enemy in comparison with several previous

[27] *Idem.*
[28] *Idem.*
[29] 15 May 1755. *C.O.* 31:28.
[30] 27 May 1755. *C.O.* 31:29.

wars. Trade involving Barbados, North America, and Europe was barely disrupted by the resumption of hostilities, and indeed the difficulties associated with the war were caused more by British success of arms than any failure to prosecute the conflict to a speedy and successful conclusion.

The French had been carefully watched for years by British naval personnel in the Indies, and after the outbreak of fighting in North America the surveillance became even more intense in order to observe any major buildup of a French striking force in the area.[31] In spite of any noticeable increase in French seapower the usual fear of isolation and privation was widespread among the Barbadians when the war commenced early in 1756, and for more than a year this dread was heightened by the presence of French privateers in and around the island.

The outbreak of the Seven Years' War in 1756 did not bring Barbados to the point of economic collapse as did the prolonged Queen Anne's War fifty years before. The new war, which crippled the commerce of the highly productive French sugar islands, was basically to the advantage of the British planters. It also renewed the anti-French feeling among the British people to the point where the use of French sugar became almost non-existent.[32]

Sugar prices reacted sharply to the war. By 1757 muscovado was averaging 37s. 1d. in London, and it rose to 42s. 5¾d. the following year.[33] The Barbadians were forced to pay higher transportation costs which detracted from the high selling price of sugar, but not sufficiently to make the war years unprofitable. In addition, the vast British fleets in the Caribbean made it a practice to provision themselves at Barbados, thus insuring the planters a ready market for their rum, which until the outbreak of hostilities had been a difficult item to sell.

The merchants, again unwilling to rely on the miserly Assembly for assistance against French depredations, supported several guard ships with their own funds, but were obliged to seek help within a few months of the start of the war. Late in 1756 the merchants were forced to petition the newly appointed Governor Charles Pinfold for additional protection against the privateers who had managed in several months time to capture or sink many supply ships and even

[31] President Ralph Weeks to Board of Trade, 24 September 1755. *C.O.* 152:46.
[32] Burn, *op. cit.*, pp. 71-72.
[33] See Table II, p. 34.

one Barbados privateer sent out to protect shipping.[34] Taking the stand that had been and was to be the touchstone of their position throughout the century, they reiterated their island's precarious trade position owing to its small size, large population, and its "great dependence upon the North American colonies as well for supplies of all sorts of provisions, as for taking off its produce".[35]

As British seapower grew in the Caribbean, the safety and well-being of the British islands was commensurately increased. By mid 1757 Governor Pinfold could report that "... the Trade of this island has suffered little from the French Privateers, partly owing to our situation, but more to the Spirit and Resolution of the merchants ...," who had outfitted their own ships to help keep the French away.[36] We must conclude from this statement that the merchants' petition for aid of the previous November had not been acted upon, but that a normal course of events had brought about an improvement in the situation.

A year later Pinfold reported that "the private brig" continued to do well, that supplies from North America were arriving in such quantity that they had to be re-exported to avoid spoilage, and that Barbados was well supplied with provisions for the coming harvest.[37] Regardless of the usual reassuring tone of most communications sent to Whitehall from colonial governors, the precise quality of this statement leads us to give it credence. Support for Pinfold's reports and for the relatively good condition of the island is to be found in the remarks of the Barbados Grand Jury late in 1758. In a letter to the governor they stated: "While our neighbours and fellow subjects of North America labor under all the calamities necessarily attending a vigorous war, we of this island ... are happy under the blessings of the most profound peace."[38]

The apparent calmness surrounding Barbados undoubtedly led to a more extensive trade in contraband merchandise during the war years than might otherwise have been possible. While several schemes were proposed to monopolize or hamper the French trade, the only restrictions were against trade in military stores with the enemy, and

[34] Petition of the Barbados merchants to Governor Charles Pinfold, 15 November 1756. *C.O.* 31:28.
[35] *Idem.*
[36] Pinfold to Board of Trade, 4 June 1757. *C.O.* 28:31, Ee. 6.
[37] Pinfold to Board of Trade, 7 January 1758. *C.O.* 28:31, Ee, 16.
[38] Remarks of the Barbados Grand Jury, 15 December 1758. *C.O.* 31:30.

a one-year embargo on all trade between the British and Dutch West Indies and South American possessions commencing in October 1756.[39] The Dutch, particularly on St. Eustatius, had become the middlemen in many of the transactions between British and French merchants during wartime, and most of the Dutch islands supported a colony of British traders who reaped large profits acting as brokers and wholesalers of a wide range of merchandise. Since it was not then by law treasonable for British subjects in neutral territory to trade with the enemy during wartime, except in military stores, the only effective way of preventing this indirect trade was by means of an embargo.[40]

Despite the British control of most of the Caribbean waters throughout the war and the imposition of embargoes and other restrictions upon trade, the movement of goods does not appear to have been unduly hampered. We need only recall that the basic loyalty of all Europeans in the Indies was to themselves and their own safety, and if this self-interest necessitated trade with the enemy the traitorous aspects of such transactions could be easily rationalized away on the grounds of self-preservation.

Trade was not even curtailed by a Barbados act in 1757 making it treason to correspond with the enemy – an act designed to harass traders dealing directly with the French.[41] Nor were the French supplied only by British and American traders during the war years. Exchanged prisoners reported that tons of Irish beef were landed on Martinique and that the French were receiving supplies from St. Eustatius and in Dutch ships from Cork.[42]

The illegal trade became so great and Barbados officials regarded it with such concern, that in 1750 a £100 reward was offered to informers on persons convicted of trading with the French on St. Vincent, and a month later the same offer was extended to accomplices

[39] In March 1756 the Duke of Newcastle suggested suspending the Navigation Acts for those neutrals who refrained from carrying French goods. It was hoped in this way to monopolize the trade of the French West Indies and to deal the French a serious financial blow by withdrawing most of the ships that normally carried off the sugar crop. The plan was never used. Add. M. 32864, f. 68. The embargo was instituted 9 October 1756. *C.O.* 31:28.

[40] See Ragatz, *op. cit.*, p. 161n.

[41] Pinfold to Board of Trade, 24 March 1757. *C.O.* 28:31, Ee. 5.

[42] Pinfold to Board of Trade, 7 January 1758. *C.O.* 28:31, Ee. 16. Pares notes in his *Colonial Blockade and Neutral Rights 1739-1763* (Oxford, 1938), that the Dutch ships came out from Holland or Cork with their cargoes chiefly on Dutch or Irish account. The provisions were sold to St. Eustatius factors and then transshipped, often without landing, to French buyers, p. 208.

who informed on their associates, plus the promise of a full pardon for their part in the operation.[43]

The preoccupation with St. Vincent had come about through insistent rumors of such a trade carried on by several local merchants and, in October of that year, the capture by a Royal Navy warship of a Barbados vessel headed for the island.[44] The trading ship had papers saying that it was destined for Guadeloupe (then in British hands), but it was in reality headed for St. Vincent to trade with the French. The owner and captain were prosecuted and imprisoned, as were all others caught engaging in the same activity.[45]

As in the wars of the previous eighty years the West Indies became a center of heavy fighting. Great fleets were sent to the area by both sides and their commanders carried orders to annex the enemy's sugar colonies, not merely to pillage them.[46] This new policy received the full support of the West Indian interests in London, although not necessarily the Barbadian.[47] Yet the planters of Barbados began to realize that their safety would be greater if Martinique and Guadeloupe were in British hands at least for the duration of the war. In the spring of 1759 Guadeloupe fell to a British fleet, but the economic effect of this seizure proved not to be what the Barbadians had expected.

The French planters were allowed to surrender on very favorable terms. They were to be neutral between France and Britain; their goods were to be admitted to British markets; their slaves were to be exempted from requisitioned work; and they were to be fully protected from seizure of their property. British planters were forbidden to settle on the island, and nothing was done to alter the French character of the colony. In addition, the French planters found a safe European and North American market for their sugars. The planters of Guadeloupe were envied alike by their associates on Martinique and by their British rivals. This was probably the kind of conquest

[43] Proclamations of Governor Pinfold, 27 November 1759, 31 December 1759. *C.O.* 31:30; *C.O.* 152:46.

[44] 1 October 1759. *C.O.* 31:30.

[45] *Idem.;* Pinfold to Board of Trade, 29 May 1760, gave evidence of the successful prosecution of six individuals for the same activities. *C.O.* 28:32. Ff. 1.

[46] Parry and Sherlock, *op. cit.*, p. 118.

[47] The views of the Barbados planters on annexing new sugar islands appear to have continually been in a state of flux, e.g., the Tobago and St. Lucia affairs earlier in the century. Within the empire, Barbados had the most to lose by the acquisition of new sugar islands, since her soil would be less productive and she was handicapped by the 4½ percent duty.

most disliked by the Barbadians; it struck directly at their profits without giving them any permanent promise of security.[48] Guadeloupe sugar began to flood the London market within six months, and the price of muscovado dropped to an average of 39s. by 1760. While this was not a low price for sugar, it did mark the first big drop in prices after a steady six year rise. Thit British planters were incensed at the terms of capitulation granted the French on Guadeloupe, but they were powerless, for the present, to do more than complain bitterly to the Board of Trade and to Parliament.

The injury was compounded in 1762 when Martinique surrendered to a fleet under Admiral Rodney. In the latter attack, "a number of" Barbados whites and 583 Negroes participated with distinction and with "inconsiderable loss" to themselves.[49]

To the annoyance of the British planters, the residents of Martinique were granted terms similar to those of Guadeloupe. Now French sugar was arriving in London from both of the captured islands. Prices slid again in the face of mounting sugar imports, muscovado touched a low of 28s. per hundredweight in 1762, fell to 25s. in 1763, and averaged only 34s. in 1764 after the French islands had been restored by the Treaty of Paris.[50]

It might seem, at first, that the decision to restore Martinique and Guadeloupe to France was made primarily at the insistence of the British planters who were naturally afraid of seeing these islands become permanent competitors for the home sugar market, for slaves, and for their excess white population.[51] Yet, even the most mercantilistic of the planters were partly converted to a policy of annexation, for they had learned, often at personal cost, what dangerous neighbors these islands could be, particularly as privateering bases.[52]

The Barbadian interest in the capture of the two chief French islands stemmed from strong feelings about their retention as British

[48] *Ibid.*, p. 120.

[49] Earl of Egremont to Pinfold, 24 January 1762. *C.O.* 28:50.; Pinfold to Egremont, 2 April 1762. *C.O.* 28:50.; *Ibid.*, 16 February 1762. The Barbados Treasury paid £3372 to the slave owners for the government's use of their services. *C.O.* 31:31.

[50] See Table II, p. 34.

[51] Burn, *op. cit.*, p. 81.

[52] Parry and Sherlock, *op. cit.*, p. 124. In 1707 the governor of St. Croix suggested capturing Martinique with ten thousand "Scots" imported for that purpose, in order to protect the sugar trade from French privateering. *C.S.P. Col.*, 1706-1708, Nos. 717, 723.

colonies at the conclusion of the war. In an address to the king on the success of his arms, it was stated in reference to Martinique that this "acquisition [should] be effectively secured by a colony truly British. The inhabitants of this island participate in many and signal advantages arising from such a situation. It also exposes us to peculiar misfortunes. The good; we acknowledge with becoming thankfulness. The evil: we humbly trust, will at least be mitigated to old and faithful subjects by Your Majesty's humanity and wisdom."[53]

Several months later Governor Pinfold in a letter to Egremont transmitted a paper on the value of keeping Martinique, "by a planter of Barbados". Pinfold stated that he differed from the author in his call to keep the island, labeling it as "premature".[54] The anonymous author called for the retention of all the islands taken from the French by conquest as "all are profitable to Great Britain". Martinique was especially desirable because of its fertility and location, and it would require "upwards of 5,000 seamen" to carry off its sugar. In French hands it would always be a menace to the British, he further argued.[55]

The writer called for the forceable evacuation of all French settlers and their replacement by an English colony. Perhaps as a hedge against additional flooding of the London sugar market as was already occurring, he suggested the raising of coffee, cocoa, and timber as the mainstays of Martinique commerce, citing the fact that even Barbados was then raising mangoes.[56] He also called for the prohibition of foreign sugar and rum in the northern colonies, and for "an unencumbered" free export of sugar to Europe, noting "perhaps the strictness of the Acts of Navigation may be partly accused for the loss of our sugar trade".[57] Finally, asking for a "diminution" of the $4\frac{1}{2}$ percent, and noting that the Barbados soil was "impoverished by long use", the writer acknowledged that there were many "English among the Dutch and Danes who [would] return if Martinique were kept".[58]

[53] Address of the Governor, Council, and Assembly of Barbados to H.M. George III, 23 March 1762. *C.O.* 31:31.

[54] Pinfold to Egremont, 20 May 1762. *C.O.* 28:50, Nos. 24-34.

[55] *Idem.*

[56] See Table II for the effect of dumping large quantities of Guadeloupe and Martinique sugars on the London market after 1759.

[57] *C.O.* 28:50, No. 29.

[58] *Ibid.*, No. 34. The Barbados Assembly passed an act to keep creditors from attaching the assets of those men who enlisted to fight the French. A creditor would risk triple damages in any attempt at seizure. *C.O.* 30:10.

Despite a scarcity of shipping in the late war years,[59] which threatened seriously to hamper the resumption of normal trade, some support for the permanent acquisition of Guadeloupe and Martinique was fortcoming in Great Britain as well as the West Indies. One writer in commenting on the North American-West Indian trade stated: "It clearly appears the convenience of this correspondence, and the benefits resulting from it are equal on both sides, and exactly suited to the temper and situation of the people by whom it is thus carried on. We cannot but plainly discern that by these new acquisitions [Martinique and Guadeloupe] in the West Indies new markets are opened."[60] He noted that the eventual profit of the sugar trade "ultimately centers with the inhabitants of Great Britain".[61]

Attempting to demolish the chief argument against acquisition used by opponents of the plan, the author remarked that "the settlement of the new islands will be no detriment to our old colonies. It seems to have been the old point in which contending writers agree, that there was a real want of more sugar land in the West Indies, and this being admitted, it would be a glaring absurdity to say that Britain is not a great gainer by these acquisitions which put so large a quantity of land fit for the cultivation of sugar into our possession."[62]

With the signing of the preliminary peace late in 1762,[63] the question placed before Parliament was essentially whether to retain all of the French West Indies, except Santo Domingo, or all of the French lands in North America, east of the Mississippi. In common terms the choice was described as retaining either Canada or the sugar islands. There were advantages to Britain regardless of the decision.[64]

For several years a considerable body of British merchants had felt that they, and Great Britain generally, were suffering a great and

[59] Letter from the Attorneys for Codrington College, Barbados, to the Reverend Dr. Daniel Burton, Secretary to the Society for the Propagation of the Gospel, London, 25 August 1763. Letter found in the Society's archives at 15 Tufton St., W.2. Hereafter cited as S.P.G. The attorneys mentioned "the present scarcity of shipping" in explaining why some of the sugar crop had not reached England.

[60] Dr. John Campbell, *Candid and Impartial Considerations on the Nature of the Sugar Trade* (London, 1763), pp. 220-222.

[61] *Idem.*

[62] *Ibid.*, p. 226.

[63] The preliminary peace with France and Spain was signed 3 November 1762. *C.O.* 31:31.

[64] Probably if the Pitt ministry had not fallen, the choice would not have had to be made, as Pitt would have endeavored to strip the Bourbons of all their overseas possessions. See Parry and Sherlock, *op. cit.*, p. 123.

unnecessary annual loss because of the inability of the British planters to expand production to a point sufficient to meet the growing demand for sugar in the United Kingdom. The most obvious remedy lay in a substantial expansion of British power and control in the West Indies.[65] From their standpoint there could be only one course of action. Guadeloupe alone, was able to produce at least one hundred thousand hogsheads of sugar annually, or nearly as much as the total production of all the British islands![66] There were those who correctly reasoned that the withdrawal of the French from North America would "ruin Britain" by lessening the northern colonists' dependence on the mother country and "promote the independence of America".[67]

In contrast to Canada, the French West Indies would bring an immediate revenue to the government and merchants alike, and the islands probably could be settled more easily with Englishmen than the vast expanse of Canada.[68] Then too, the permanent acquisition of Guadeloupe and Martinique would relieve Britain of one of her heaviest economic burdens, the high cost of sugar. The truth of this statement was aptly demonstrated by the impact made by the Guadeloupe sugars on London selling prices during the period from 1759 to 1762. Finally, by keeping the French islands and occupying the neutral islands of the West Indies, Britain would have gained a virtual monopoly of sugar production. This, combined with her large fleet of merchant ships, would insure complete dominance for Britain in the distribution and sale of a large majority of the world's sugar.

The West Indies, on the other hand, would always be weak, and dependent upon outside help for provisions, access to markets, and defense from attack. Canada would, in time, probably become a much larger market for British manufactures than any of the West Indian islands. In this respect the northern colonies were already far more important than the West Indies.[69] Mainland colonies whose people, however poor, were nearly all free and white, naturally had more need for consumer products than islands full of slaves.[70] While it was true that the northern colonies might one day establish industries of

[65] Pitman, *op. cit.*, p. 345.

[66] *Idem.*

[67] "A Letter From A Gentleman in Guadeloupe to His Friend in London, August 1760", Pitman *op. cit.*, p. 346.

[68] Parry and Sherlock, *op. cit.*, p. 124.

[69] Richard Pares, *War and Trade in the West Indies 1739-1763* (Oxford, 1936), pp. 217-218.

[70] *Idem.*

their own, most economic writers of the period were convinced that this would not occur for many years.[71] Economically, the weight of the argument was probably on the side of keeping the French islands, but economic considerations did not decide the issue at the peace table. Furthermore, the popular viewpoint. which the British statesmen had to acknowledge, was that the prime reason for Britain's entry into the war was to drive the French out of Canada in order to prevent all future wars on the North American continent.[72]

The peace treaty was carried by an overwhelming majority in the House of Commons. The vote of the planters in Commons was most certainly split on the question. Perhaps there was a division between "saturated" planters and unsaturated.[73] The difference between a "saturated" and an unsaturated planter lay in the greater investment of capital, and the willingness or need of the latter to expand. Since Barbados had been fully planted for almost one hundred years, the acquisition of other islands suitable for sugar planting remained the only way to accomplish needed expansion. The saturated planters probably were older men who had long since given up any thought of enlarging their interests, and had retired to England leaving the operation of their estates to agents and overseers.

Nobody advised the ministers to keep Canada more strongly than Rose Fuller and William Bockford, the two most important and vocal planters in British politics.[74] Both men would be classed as "saturated" planters. The lesson they had learned when Guadeloupe and, later, Martinique sugars broke the London market was undoubtedly still too vivid in their memory to allow them to support any move for the retention of the French sugar islands, the military consequences notwithstanding. The dilemma of the Barbadians is very clearly stated in a letter from Admiral Rodney to Lord Lyttleton written in 1762.

> The planters are divided between avarice and fear, they think if Martinique is retained, they will be obliged to lower the price of their sugars. On the other hand, if it is given up, they fear the loss of their own plantations in case of another war, and that the French will overrun them before they can receive succours from Europe, which as I said before, they may easily do, and the example of this war has taught them a lesson, which I fancy they will never forget.[75]

[71] *Idem.*

[72] *Ibid.*, p. 219.

[73] L. B. Namier, *England in the Age of the American Revolution* (London, 1930), p. 322.

[74] Pares, *War and Trade in the West Indies*, p. 219.

[75] Rodney to Lyttleton, 29 June 1762, cited in *Ibid.*, p. 223.

Canada and the neutral islands proved to be fertile fields for British capital and enterprise in the years to come, and in North America the French threat against the British colonies was finally ended. The only drawback was that these acquisitions were not likely to help repay the huge British war debt by bringing in immediate revenue as the retention of Martinique and Guadeloupe would have done.

When news of the final settlement reached Barbados it was greeted with a profound sense of relief by all of the inhabitants who had labored under the handicaps of war for seven years.[76] Yet there were many who viewed the peace terms as portentous. Governor Pinfold and his Council immediately sent congratulations to George III on the successful conclusion of the fighting, but the document was not signed by any members of the Barbados Assembly who had composed their own message to their sovereign.

Pinfold remarked that, "Great care was taken to pen this address in general terms, to induce those who disliked some articles of the treaty to write in thanks to a general peace always beneficial to an island dependent on commerce. But notwithstanding this caution the House of Assembly could not be persuaded to join the Governor and Council in that part relative to the peace."[77] In fact, the Assembly refused to extend congratulations in irritation over the terms of peace. Using the third person in reference to itself, the Assembly document stated: "But the Assembly cannot consent to [offer] their congratulations on the peace, as they would be to contradict the truth of their sincerest sentiments upon the subject."[78]

The reaction of the king and his ministers is not recorded, if indeed they were concerned at all with the mouthings of a distant Assembly. We cannot, however, doubt the sincerity of the Assembly's action under the circumstances surrounding the restitution of the captured French islands. By way of explanation for its action the Assembly wrote Governor Pinfold expressing its pleasure at the successful conquest of the French islands and Martinique especially, but remarking

> How then can we behold the restitution of this important conquest with that of so many others near it as must add considerably to its weight and influence in the scale of power against us — and all of them restored in a condition that must make them the most formidable rivals during a peace, as well as the most destructive foes in any future war! How can we turn

[76] Peace was proclaimed 24 June 1763. *C.O.* 28:50, Nos. 51.

[77] Pinfold to Egremont, 16 July 1763. *C.O.* 28:50, Nos. 53-54.; Governor and Barbados Council to H.M. George III, 12 July 1763. *C.O.* 31:31.

[78] Barbados Assembly to H.M. George III, 16 July 1763. *C.O.* 28:50, No. 56.

our eyes to this unfortunate prospect for Barbados and not find the joy which has been carried to the throne by so many other bodies of our fellow subjects on the peace unhappily checked within the bosom of our own community!

Whatever may have been the proper business and felicity of most other countries on a reestablishment of peace, it is the part of wisdom and good policy in the people of this island, we acknowledge, to provide for their defense and guard in the best manner they are able against another war, which more than possible, we cannot but consider as the most probable event, and which too, if we measure by the few years only that may be necessary to restore the ancient enemies of our kingdom to their wanted strength (the eternal spring of their ambition), we can hardly flatter ourselves is so far distant as your excellency in your generous concern for our security is desposed to place it.[79]

The British Caribbean conquests were not all bargained away at the peace table. Grenada, Tobago, Dominica, St. Vincent, and the Grenadines were retained as spoils of war, or perhaps to avoid repeating the neutrality mistake of Aix-la-Chapelle. Cuba was returned to Spain in exchange for control of Florida, and Britain remained content in limiting her major gains to India and Canada.

The motivation behind the government's move to retain only part of the French empire, won at high cost by force of arms, has long been the subject of academic debate. Comparison of the relative merits of Canada and the French sugar islands as colonies leads one to the quick (and correct) assumption that if the choice had been made on the immediate value of the two, the sugar islands would have been retained. History has proven the correctness of the other choice, but the necessity of Britain's making a choice at all was not due to West Indian pressure. Nor do the facts support the accepted theory that it was the West India interest's opposition to a dilution of their monopoly rights that forced the Burke government to accede to the return of Martinique and Guadeloupe to France.[80]

Recent research has shown that it was a desire for peace at any price and an unwillingness to weaken France too severely as a continental power that led to the British compromise at the Treaty of Paris. Furthermore, the forceful and headstrong role played by George III in the peace settlement precluded the emergence of any other pressure group to a position of dominance in the negotiations, and while these groups did exist representing all shades of interest, their

[79] Barbados Assembly to Governor Pinfold, 20 September 1763. *C.O.* 31:31.
[80] See Ragatz, *op. cit.*, pp. 111-112, for a statement of this position.

efforts were foredoomed to be of little avail by the intrangency of the king.

To be sure there is adequate evidence of strong pressure on Parliament and on the ministers of George III by the West Indian Committee and other groups of "saturated" planters residing in London to return the captured French islands, but we can not accept these men as typical planters nor their arguments as representative of current West Indian opinion.[81] These men concerned only with profits wrung with difficulty out of a trade monopoly within the empire could not be expected to share the feelings of their fellow planters in the islands, and perhaps may be excused for their shortsighted stand. It is hard to conceive that it was this pressure alone that brought about the return of the French islands, especially in view of the determined opposition from men of position and authority living in the Caribbean.

There is considerable evidence of strong support within the empire for the retention of Martinique and Guadeloupe as early as 1760. An anonymous pamphleteer in either 1760 or 1761 wrote: "I am for retaining all our American conquests, and even for insisting upon Martinico, that sepulchre of our merchant men, twelve hundred of which have been carried into that island since the beginning of the war."[82] In his pamphlet "Considerations on the Present German War", Israel Mauduit wrote that a further continuance of the war in Europe was a waste, and that France could be harmed easier by capturing her colonies, "not useless ones on the Mississippi, but by seizing the French islands and holding their whole West India trade in deposit for Hanover".[83]

Mauduit also accused William Pitt of being unduly influenced by a Mr. Beckford, a Jamaica planter residing in London and a Member of Parliament. As early as 1759 Beckford spoke earnestly of the necessity to return Guadeloupe to the French out of fear, according to Mauduit, that its retention would be detrimental to his sugar lands in Jamaica.[84] There is some evidence that Pitt, for one reason or

[81] For a summation of the saturated planter position, i.e., that espoused by the London planter groups, see G. L. Beer, *British Colonial Policy, 1754-65* (New York, 1933), Chapter XIII, and F. W. Pitman, *op. cit.*, Chapter XIV.

[82] William L. Grant, "Canada Versus Guadeloupe, An Episode of the Seven Years' War", *American Historical Review*, July 1912, pp. 735-743.

[83] Israel Mauduit, *Considerations on the Present German War* (London, 1761), 4th ed., p. 137.

[84] *Ibid.*

another, had become less sure in his aggressiveness toward the French, for in 1760 he remarked, "a nation may overconquer itself, and by being fed with more conquests than it can digest, may have the overplus turn to surfeit and disease instead of nourishment".[85]

Some critics of the peace correctly divined the effect that the expulsion of the French from Canada would have on the thirteen colonies in terms of removing colonial dependence on British arms, and correctly predicted an increase in the northern colonists disregard for the Acts of Trade in their dealings with the French West Indies. Many argued for a proportioned empire, half temperate and half tropical, with both parts in balance.[86] The final result could not be cheered by discerning men.

The expression of satisfaction over the retention of the lesser French islands composed by the Barbados Council in 1764 affords us a further example of the concensus which prevailed in the Indies on the subject. The document stated:

> The ceded islands acquired by the vigor of H.M. arms, preserved by the wisdom of his councils; while they enlarge H.M. extensive Dominions, must necessarily increase the commerce of our mother country, and open new veins of wealth to our fellow subjects, from hence the necessary burdens of the late expensive, but successful war will be alleviated, from hence too, shall we, the better be enabled to repel the encroachments of a future aspiring invader.[87]

The resident planters, mostly men with hopes of expanding their operations, tended to view the retention of the French islands as a logical and necessary step for the expansion of British Caribbean interests — the least of which might be the enlargement of their own holdings, and as a vital precaution against further French economic and military encroachments upon themselves in the future. A realistic survey of West Indian thought on the eve of 1764 reveals a widespread dissatisfaction with the terms of peace so recently concluded at Paris. Once again the British West Indies would be forced to pay the price exacted by the machinations of politics in the mother country over which they exerted but slight control.

[85] Grant, *op. cit.*, pp. 742-743.

[86] *Ibid.*, p. 741.

[87] Barbados Council to Governor Pinfold, 30 October 1764. *C.O.* 31:31. Two years earlier Pinfold had written to the Board of Trade that the capture of Martinique gave the citizens of Barbados a feeling of securtiy. 30 May 1762. *C.O.* 28:32, Ff. 24.

IV

REALIGNMENT

The national debt of Great Britain which had been approximately £60,000,000 at the start of the Seven Years' War in 1756 had more than doubled to £130,000,000 at its conclusion. Added to this increase in indebtedness was the burden of maintaining extensive acquisitions won by the force of British arms in two hemispheres. The annual cost of supporting the civil and military establishments in America alone had risen from some £70,000 in 1748 to well over £350,000 by 1764.[1]

Offsetting this staggering financial burden was the singularly robust economic condition of the empire at the close of the war. Canada, India, and the former neutral islands proved to be fertile fields for British capital and enterprise. The only drawback was that these acquisitions were not likely to help repay the huge war debt by bringing in immediate revenue as the retention of Martinique and Guadeloupe would have done. All of the areas – particularly Canada – would need a number of years and considerable investment of capital before they could approach the net worth of the two large French islands. Thus wisdom dictated that taxation of trade alone would not suffice in the task of supporting the empire.

Nonetheless a pressing need for additional funds resulted in the passage of the Revenue Act of 1764. The act sprang from dual motives: to provide revenue, and to insure the continued flow of tax moneys by strengthening the Acts of Trade. When peace arrived the West Indian planters again petitioned that trade between the mainland colonists and the French sugar islands be prohibited or curtailed by increasing the molasses duties. Parliament acceded neither to this argument nor to the northern plea for the abolition of all duties on foreign sugars. More concerned with financial and administrative affairs than with orthodox mercantilism in what was basically an

[1] Samuel Eliot Morison and Henry Steele Commager, *The Growth of the American Republic,* I (New York, 1942), p. 146; George L. Beer, *op. cit.*, pp. 267-268.

extension of the Molasses Act, it lowered the duty from 6d. to 3d. per gallon and took steps to insure that the act would be properly enforced.

Action of some sort was long overdue for the Act of 1733 had long ceased to serve as a useful tool of either taxation or regulation. In 1763 the Commissioner of Customs reported that

> With respect to the duties laid by the 6 of George II the Molasses Act upon sugar, rum, and molasses imported from foreign colonies into the British American colonies, it appears to us from the smallness of the sum collected from these duties and from other evidence, that they have been for the most part either wholly evaded, or fraudulently compounded . . .[2]

Calling for an improvement in the collection procedures, the Commissioner noted that the northern colonists would probably continue to import most of their sugar from the French West Indies, "where they will be likely to obtain the cheapest rate . . ."[3]

The absence of any protest against the Act of 1764 on the part of the West Indian planters gives credence to the accepted thesis that the planter interests in Parliament generally supported the measure in lieu of an all-out prohibition of trade in foreign sugar. Sugar prices had dropped twenty-five percent from their 1762 high of 40s., and any attempt to remedy what might become a prolonged price break would be looked upon with favor by the West Indians.[4]

The sword of taxation however carried a double edge – not only were the customs procedures tightened-up, but additional duties were laid upon the importation of luxuries such as wines, silks, and linens, while drawbacks (rebates) on most European goods re-exported from Britain to the colonies were abolished. The net result of a well-functioning act would be wholly favorable only to the Exchequer.

The results were unsatisfactory on both sides of the Atlantic. Rather than submit to the new act, most of the colonial merchants improved upon their former methods of evasion. The British government found that the taxes brought in very little money, and that the costs of enforcement were not commensurate with the slight increase in revenue brought about by the measure. Added pressure was brought upon the government by many British merchants to find a substitute

[2] Commissioner of Customs to Board of Trade, 16 September 1763. Add. M. 8133C ff. 85-87.

[3] *Idem.*

[4] See Table II, p. 34. The opposite feelings were held by the refiner's association in England. Low prices meant an end to the unnaturally high prices paid by the refiners for sugar during the war years, and a chance to increase their profits at long last.

method of taxation. Already concerned with the plight of their American debtors and fearful lest the entire structure of colonial finance collapse, thus rendering their debts uncollectable, the merchants urged caution upon the Grenville ministry.

Indirect taxation of trade having failed as a means of raising the needed revenue, a direct method of taxation was decided upon and embodied in the famous Stamp Act of 1765. The idea of a stamp tax was not novel. Such a tax had long been in use in Britain and its application in the American colonies had often been proposed.[5]

The Act provided for revenue stamps costing from ½d. to 20 s. sterling to be affixed to all newspapers, broadsides (leaflets), pamphlets, licenses, commercial bills, notes and bonds, almanacs, legal documents, and a number of other similar papers. All of the revenue collected was to be spent solely in the colonies for their defense, and offenses against the Act were to be tried in the Admiralty Courts.[6] The British stamp duty brought in approximately £300,000 yearly. Its extension to America was calculated to raise an additional £10,000–£50,000 from the British West Indies alone.[7]

News of the passage of the Act in March of 1765 and the beginning of stamp sales in November was greeted with less hostility on Barbados than in the thirteen northern colonies, even though the Act worked no less of a hardship upon the Barbadians than upon their northern brethern. The tendency was to regard the Stamp Act as merely one more of a series of "imposts and burdens" laid upon the planters, and the Barbadians took no particular comfort in the knowledge that the tax had been applied indiscriminately throughout British America.

In Barbados as in the northern colonies the imposition of the Stamp Act raised a constitutional issue, centered on the question of virtual representation in the British Parliament – representation of classes and interests rather than by locality. The Barbados Assembly had as early as 1740 reaffirmed its right to be the sole agency for

[5] All legal documents and most commercial paper (checks, invoices, receipts, etc.) must still carry revenue stamps from two pence upwards to twenty pounds in the United Kingdom.

[6] Morison and Commager, *op. cit.*, p. 149.

[7] George L. Beer, *op. cit.*, p. 285-286, states that the measure was designed to raise £60,000 to £100,000 in North America and the West Indies. Sir Winston Churchill in his *History of the English Speaking Peoples*, III (London, 1957), states that the Act's extension to America was only expected to raise another £50,000 – thus the figure of £10,000 for the British West Indies.

levying taxes, stating that taxes could not be "laid upon the inhabitants of this island without the consent of their representatives", nor would it permit any alterations to be made in a bill concerning money passed by it.[8]

Expressing practically the same view as that taken by the American Stamp Act Congress – that no taxes ever have been, or can be, constitutionally imposed on the various colonies, except by their respective legislatures – the Barbados Assembly addressed Governor Pinfold:

> [The people] feel the burden of this impost heavy on their properties. You are far more sensible of the oppressive doctrine that supports it and bears down their dearest liberties. To be subject to no internal taxation of government, but what is authorized by the representative body of each society in concert with the representative of the crown presiding over it, is a privilege which we imagined the subjects of Great Britain had been particularly entitled to in every settlement, however distant, of the British Empire as a birthright and blessing indeed capable of making every settlement, even the most distant of that Empire grateful to a British spirit. It was under the shade of this privilege at least that our ancestors first ventured forth to toil and establish themselves as a colony in this sultry clime. And must their posterity yet guiltless and unoffending be now left exposed by the loss of it to reap in bitterness the fruits of their success?
>
> Long have we paid in customs on our commodities at home and in the duties collected on them here a large and grateful tribute to the Crown. Hard then is our lot in these days of peace and national prosperity to be charged with an additional load of taxes, and these too aggravated by the manner of imposing them, equally unmerited as unnecessary.[9]

At this point the Assembly's attack upon the Act failed to measure up to the outspoken declaration of the New York congress as the Barbadians disavowed those who would resort to forceful measures in opposition to a "legal ordinance" of Parliament. The address continued

> But we forbear! We know it is your Excellencys duty to see this act observed and we do not forget that it is ours to show the due submission. To submit without contention to every legal ordinance of our mother country is indeed a duty which the loyal inhabitants of this country never can renounce, but to submit to such an ordinance as this without complaint would be, if possible, to deserve the evil we deplore.[10]

Here was the basic difference between the northern colonies and

[8] 26 November 1740. *C.O.* 31:22.

[9] Barbados Assembly to Governor Pinfold, 26 November 1765. *C.O.* 31:32; *C.O.* 31:33.

[10] *Idem.*

Barbadas Feb. 21. 1766

My Lords.

The Favor of Yr. Lordships 23. Augt. was received in Due time but having then nothing of consequence to communicate for his Majestys Service I delayed my answer till I might transmit Information worthy your Lordships Notice: Near four Months are now elapsed since the Commencement of the Stamp Duty, and it is with a very peculiar Joy & Satisfaction that I am able to acquaint yr. Lordships all here has been Quiet & Easy; A Ready Obedience has been paid to the Act of the British Parliament, which does honor to the Inhabitants; and your Lordships Sense of Justice will I am assured induce you to represent to his Majesty in proper terms the repeated Instance of the Dutiful & Loyal conduct of the Inhabitants of Barbados: especially as their North American Correspondents have spared neither Threats, or Entreaties to persuade us to imitate their outrageous and Rebellious Conduct: I entertain the firmest hopes his Majestys Ministers will have no trouble from this Colony on this Subject, & that it will be as much in my power, as it is my Inclination & Duty to maintain the public tranquillity.

The Death of Mr. John Frere has made a Vacancy in his Majestys Council. By several Letters to yr. Lordships Board I have recommended Mr. Jonathan Worrel as a proper Successor. I still entertain the same Opinion of that Gentleman, he is now in England, and the public service (as several Members are absent) requires the presence of the Gentleman whom his Majesty shall be graciously pleased to appoint to supply this Vacancy, I can therefore only mention him to yr. Lordships on a supposition that he assures yr. Lordships of his Speedy return to Barbados.

But in case this does not suit his Inclinations

I Humbly beg Leave in pursuance of the Royal Instruction to lay before yr. Lordships the Names of three Gentlemen resident in the Island, Richard Cobham, Henry Beckles, Samuel Husbands, the first to succeed Mr. John Greene Deceased the others to be inserted in yr. Lordships Book proper to supply future Vacancies: they are Gentlemen of Abilities, Good Estates, & well affected to his Majestys Person & Government: I Doubt not but yr. Lordships in this respect will honor me with the same Confidence as yr. Predecessors have since I have been ~~[illegible]~~ entrusted with the Government, & adopt their Opinion that the Governor who has resided here so many years ought to know the Abilities of the Inhabitants, & is the Most proper to name those who are most capable of executing his Majestys Commands: I take the Liberty to mention this more fully as I am apprehensive Recommendations will be offered ~~[illegible]~~ of Others who in my Opinion are Totally improper to be entrusted in matters of Government.

His Majesty having been Graciously pleased in Compliance with my Humble Request to grant me Leave to be absent from my Government for one Year for the Settlement of my private Affairs, I take this Oportunity to inform yr. Lordships that I propose to avail my self of the Royal permission & to embark for England in the Month of May: In Obedience to the Royal Instruction I shall commit the Administration to the Eldest Resident Member of Council. On my Arrival I shall hasten to pay my Duty to yr. Lordships & shall esteem it a great Happiness to have in any part of my Administration merited yr. Approbation.

I have the Honor to be with the Greatest Regard & Respect yr. Lordships most Obedient Humble Servant

Chas. Pinfold

those in the West Indies. While the logic of the Constitutional arguments against the home government's program of imperial reorganization might well strike a responsive cord among thinking colonists throughout British America, their forthcoming views as to what, if anything, should be done by way of opposing the plan were widely varied. The violence of Massachusetts and the other northern colonies expressed in the fury of countless mobs acting to nullify the Act was not found in Barbados, nor did West Indian opposition to the stamps ever reach the intensity of that shown on the North American continent.

On Barbados the Act was obeyed from its inception in November 1765. On several occasions the supply of stamps even became dangerously low when their use exceeded expectations.[11] The Barbadians were not free from pressure to take a more positive stand against the Act however. In February Governor Pinfold reported that though the Act had been in force for three months and though he and his staff had experienced no difficulty in the distribution of stamps "the North Americans have in their letters spared neither threats or entreaties to persuade us to imitate their outrageous and Rebellious Conduct".[12]

The Assembly still seethed at the insult to its prerogatives and many members of the lower house in active correspondence with mainland agitators in the natural course of their business dealings were only with great difficulty able to endure the urging of those who proposed that they follow the action of the Americans. In January 1766, the Assembly suggested that the Council join them in presenting a remonstrance to the king against the Stamp Act, but when the Council refused to take a strong stand the matter was dropped.[13]

News of the repeal of the Stamp Act was received with considerable joy and a joint message of approval was sent to the king by the Assembly and the now bold Council.[14] Repeal had been forced by the American boycott of British goods during the last half of 1765, and in turn by British merchants faced with grave losses because of their shrinking markets. For the second time in as many years the Americans had successfully defied the authority of Parliament with

[11] Pinfold to the Earl of Halifax, 17 December 1765. *C.O.* 28:50, no. 68.

[12] Pinfold to Board of Trade, 21 February 1766. *C.O.* 28:32, Ff. 68; *C.O.* 28:50, no. 118.

[13] 2 January 1766. *C.O.* 31:33.

[14] 10-12 June 1766. *C.O.* 31:33. The message was not found

but little or no assistance from their fellow subjects in the Indies.

A clear pattern of abject neutrality in the face of the mounting power struggle then taking place on the North American continent was beginning to emerge in the responses of the West Indians to the shifting currents of controversy. It was, perhaps, a neutrality born out of a realization of planter dependence upon others for their survival as a society; perhaps it was a facet of inherent planter conservatism not wishing to destroy the existing order of things. Perhaps too, it was the mark of the impotency of political thought subtly nourished through generations of single-minded devotion to the cause of sugar. Whatever the reason, the stream of political leadership ran shallow throughout the Indies in the decade of turbulence preceding the American Revolution. West Indian society afforded little room for unorthodoxy in any form. There could be no broad base of public support for a man with the message of Samuel Adams, James Otis, or Christopher Gadsden in colonies eighty to ninety percent slave. There could be no non-importation agreements backed by a powerful merchants association on islands that had to import to live.

West Indian Assemblies, where a Patrick Henry or an Otis might have been found had circumstances been different, were the most politically astute groups in the Caribbean. But they were for the most part composed of realistic men who knew only too well the limitations imposed upon them and their islands by economics and geography. Regardless of their personal sympathies these men were powerless to act in a positive manner in support of the American radical point of view, and by not acting, they gave indirect support to the established order. The ambivalence of many government officials toward imperial reorganization and the events of 1764 and 1765 can be seen in an address of the Barbados Council written six months after the repeal of the Stamp Act.

> We exult that the conduct pursued by us during the force of the Stamp Act received the royal sanction; while our loyalty dictated obedience, our hopes extended themselves to the repeal of a measure we trusted His Majesty's parental care would insure to us when found oppressive.[15]

By way of explanation for their beliefs the Council noted that

> The part of submission which was taken by this colony in that memorial trial of their obedience by the late Stamp Act was indeed agreeable to the

[15] Barbados Council to President Rous, 7 January 1767. *C.O.* 31:33.

soundest policy in our state, as well as the result of a principle, not easily to be shaken by the first, though too well founded cause of general discontent. Happy are we then to find the confidence we reposed on that occasion in the wisdom of a righteous Parliament and the goodness of a gracious sovereign, so justly recompensed by a total release from the oppressive burden.[16]

The issue of internal taxation without representation is not mentioned in the address, the Council members preferring instead to base their opposition to the measure upon the vague charge of its having caused "general discontent" in the colony.

Save for one message to the king *after* the repeal of the Stamp Act, there was not a single challenge or protest filed during the course of its enactment or application by the legislative leadership of Barbados. The planter dominated Assembly and Council could ill-afford the antagonize Parliament, for to do so would compromise their precarious position as the beneficiaries of legislation favorable to sugar.

Thanks largely to American aggressiveness the stamp ordeal ended less than six months after it started. A contemporary writer noted that "During the few months it was in force, the sum of £2,500 was collected at Barbados, and remitted to England" – a remarkable sum for such a brief period.[17]

Throughout the period Parliament was continually pressed by British planters living in England who had formed an organization together with West Indian merchants for the promotion of their interests. Taking the name of the West India Committee the group met informally as the need dictated and sought to influence legislation, regulate conditions of the sale and handling of sugar, and in general advance the interests of their product.[18]

[16] *Idem.*

[17] George Frere, *A Short History of Barbados* (London, 1768), p. 76. The figure is suspect owing to Frere's well known bias toward Barbados, and on the grounds of the more accurate estimate of £10,000 in tax revenues to be collected from *all* the British West Indies made by the Exchequer. If Barbados with only twenty percent of the white population of Jamaica were able to remit £5,000 yearly to the government, then it would seem possible for the two islands alone to raise nearly £30,000 per year in Stamp Act revenues. This seems highly unlikely.

[18] Evidence is lacking as to the exact date of the Committee's formation, but it is known that as early as the 1730's a number of London planters had formed an organization known as the Planters' Club for the promotion of common interests. Add. M. 12431, ff. 116-117, 120-1. By 1760 the group had expanded its activities and membership to include not only planters but those merchants trading in West Indian produce. The records of the Committee are complete only from 1769,

Seizing the opportunity afforded by the repeal of the Stamp Act, the Committee proposed: (1) removal of all duties upon British sugar imported into North America, (2) continuance of the 5s. duty per hundredweight on all foreign sugars imported into North America, (3) removal of the 7s. duty per hundredweight on British-grown coffee, (4) classifying all sugars imported by Great Britain from North America as foreign, (5) establishment of a free port in Jamaica for Spanish ships.[19]

Proposals of this nature were common enough during the latter half of the eighteenth century and serve only to give us an insight into the thinking of the planter interests. Parliament burdened with matters of more vital concern to the commonwealth was not as receptive to these memorials as it had once been, giving fresh evidence of the relative decline of planter influence and importance within the empire.

Faced with an unwillingness or an inability to give voice to their views on the political and taxation policies of the home government, and by a loss of influence within the councils of government, the West Indians withdrew into the role of spectators in the developing struggle between their fellow colonists in North America and the mother country.[20] The role could not have been to their liking for it was easy to see that regardless of the course of events fractricidal conflict would undoubtedly send adverse repercussions throughout the empire to the detriment of all. Yet during the whole progress of the dispute, the legislature of Barbados maintained a respectful silence, unwilling to add to the "perplexities of the ministry . . ., or conscious that no application of theirs would be regarded when interests of far greater national importance depended upon the issue of the contest".[21]

---

and we must rely on indirect evidence for knowledge of the organization's earlier activities, For a brief history of the various planter and merchant groups established prior to the Committee see: Dame Lillian Penson, *The Colonial Agents of the British West Indies* (London, 1924), Chaps. IX, X. A more detailed history of the West India Committee is Douglas Hall, *The West India Committee, A Historical Outline* (unpublished MS London, 1956), available at the West India Society offices, 1 Norfolk Street, London, W.C. 2.

[19] 10 March, 8 May 1766. Add. M. 33030 f. 206, f. 245.

[20] The Barbados Assembly occasionally tugged at the bonds of restraint placed upon it by executive fiat. In 1767 the assembly demanded "that we and our servants may be free in our persons and estates from arrests and other disturbances; that in our debates liberty and freedom of speech be allowed us" [as is the custom in Parliament]. 3 June 1767. *C.O.* 31:34. The request was granted. *Ibid.*, 4 August 1767.

[21] John Poyer, *The History of Barbados, 1605-1801* (London, 1808), pp. 574-576.

Although participation in the developing North American crisis had been denied them, the Barbadians became enmeshed in a new power struggle with French interests within a year of the Treaty of Paris. Denied their former positions in the neutral islands by the peace settlement, the French began to colonize along the South American coast to the East of the Dutch settlement at Paramaribo.[22]

Any hostile base to windward of Barbados would always be viewed with some apprehension for, as the Barbadians correctly surmised, their safety in previous wars was in large measure due to the inability of an enemy to mount an attack upon the island against the prevailing current and winds. The French settlement at Cayenne was especially alarming, for the relative scarcity of British shipping along the South American coast would make it easy for the French to assemble a large striking force without detection.[23]

In the near future however the Cayenne settlement gave promise of being more of a trade nuisance than a source of potential military danger. In September 1765 a British naval captain reported the colony hard hit by disease and suffering for want of provisions. "I think we need not be under any apprehensions at any of our islands of a vessel from the French from the province of Guianna for many years if ever", he optimistically wrote to Governor Pinfold.[24] It was also reported that the Cayenne Governor admitted the loss of 10,000 of the original 14,000 settlers to disease in the steamy wilderness.[25]

In spite of their losses the French had come to stay and were already engaged in an extensive reciprocal trade with North American merchants from Philadelphia and other northern ports. Proof of illicit trade was furnished with the capture by a British warship early in 1765 of the brigantine "Chance", a Philadelphia ship out of North Carolina with a cargo of provisions destined for Cayenne.[26]

The ship carried two sets of papers: false ones stating her destination to be Barbados, and correct ones listing Cayenne as her goal. A bill of lading found on board revealed the existence of a contract

[22] The area now known as French Guiana.

[23] Pinfold to Board of Trade, 23 February 1765. *C.O.* 28:32, Ff. 53. Navy men estimated that the voyage from Cayenne to Barbados would take only 8 to 10 days and would pose a serious threat to Barbados in a future war. *Idem.; C.O.* 28:50, no. 83.

[24] Captain Knowles to Pinfold, 19 September 1765. *C.O.* 28:50, nos. 113-114.

[25] 2 October 1765. *C.O.* 31:33.

[26] 12 March 1765. *C.O.* 31:31; Pinfold to the Earl of Halifax, 23 March 1765. *C.O.* 28:50, no. 89; 12 March 1765. *C.O.* 28:50, no. 94.

between the ship's owners and the French to supply their South American settlement with provisions. The "Chance" carried beef, wheat, livestock, pitch, tar, and turpentine making her seizure one of considerable value for her captors.[27]

Brought to Barbados and condemned by the courts for violating the Navigation Acts, the ship focused the attention of the Barbadians upon the renewed danger of French aggression and the independent course of action in economic and political affairs still pursued by the American colonists. Governor Pinfold wrote to the Board of Trade that

> these transactions of the Northern Colonies to aid and assist a French settlement which may here after be prejudicial to these islands, and the clandestine manner of carrying on this trade by fictitious papers seemed to me a matter worthy of your Lords help and consideration.[28]

The facts were well known to British officials, but since they were already in possession of the French government's promise not to engage in any trading activity other than that authorized by the Acts, there was little that could easily be done to remedy the situation short of a complete change in French policy or American economic circumstances. Only with the latter could the home government play a positive role by enacting or repealing measures so as to moderate the imbalance of colonial trade from North America.

Such action, even willingly undertaken, would be slow in redressing years of accumulated restrictions, bounties, drawbacks, and prohibitions that had channeled colonial trade into its existing pattern. It was obvious that the British West Indies would continue to suffer a loss of trade and revenue until these inequities could be resolved. It was equally obvious that relief could not be expected from a monarch whose chief concern was the enhancement of the royal prerogatives, or from a Parliament embroiled in the increasing complexities of administering the largest colonial empire in the world.

French officials refused to become implicated in the matter, preferring instead to remain decorously neutral. While proclaiming at every opportunity their adherence to the official policy of discouraging foreign trade, most French authorities in the Indies overtly encouraged such trade, particularly with North America, as a matter of

[27] It was customary to reward the officers and crew of navy ships with a percentage of the condemnation value of any ship seized by them and found to be in violation of the Acts of Trade.

[28] Pinfold to the Earl of Halifax, 23 March 1765. *C.O.* 28:50, no. 89.

necessity. Unable to supply themselves with adequate provisions from within their own commonwealth or to market their full production of sugars, it became essential for the planters to cultivate the growing market in British North America. If this had been the case twenty years earlier, it became vital after 1763.[29]

In a move designed to strengthen the trade position of the British islands in general, Parliament in 1766 authorized the establishment of free ports on Dominica and Jamaica.[30] Selected because of their favored location astride the French and Spanish shipping lanes, these islands soon showed marked increases in trade while simultaneously injuring many of their own planters who could no longer compete in the local market with cheap foreign sugars.

The planters of Dominica were especially hard hit for like most other British planters they suffered from the twin ills of a single crop and inefficient methods of production, while Jamaica with its greater size and diversity of crops continued to prosper and grow at an accelerated rate. Already secure in its position as the most important British colony in the West Indies by 1766, the added impetus of free trade covering a wide spectrum of goods would soon enable Jamaica to equal and then better the trade totals from the rest of the British islands combined![31]

This partial departure by Parliament from previous colonial policy must have struck the Barbadians as the beginning of a new phase in imperial planning, for the impact of the free ports on the economies of Dominica and Jamaica was closely studied from the first. The Barbados merchants were, of course, keenly aware of the advantages accorded to their compatriots on the chosen islands and almost from the beginning supported a movement to have Bridgetown declared a free port. The Barbados planters however were just as aware of the plight of the Dominican planters and after their initial pleasure with the implications of the new law tended to view the idea of a free port for Barbados with reservation.

[29] In 1765 Governor Gousand of Martinique reiterated his compliance with his king's orders not to trade with foreign ships; but he acknowledged that he did allow them to pass nearby. Letter from Governor Gousand to Pinfold, 2 October 1765. *C.O.* 31:33.

[30] Whitehall, 11 July 1766. *C.O.* 31:32. For a thorough presentation of the free port bill in Parliament, and its subsequent effect on Jamaica and Dominica see Lawrence H. Gipson, *The British Empire Before The American Revolution*, IX (New York, 1956), pp. 245-254.

[31] Trade statistics support these statements as early 1769.

For several years the question was debated in the colony, and in 1773 a resolution was introduced in the Assembly calling for the establishment of a free port in Barbados. Supported by the merchants and shipping interests the bill faced determined opposition from a majority of planters. Secure in the knowledge that the measure enjoyed the support of Governor Hay, and that French economic competition continued to increase to the detriment of Barbados, its proponents were optimistic.[32]

Planter interests in the Assembly felt that passage of the bill would deny protection to their products if similar products were freely imported as was the case on Dominica. It was finally amended to prohibit the importation of rum, sugar, molasses, aloes, tobacco, and ginger, and the exportation of lumber, pitch, tar, tobacco, and turpentine.[33] The planters thus weakened the measure by amendment to the point of ineffectiveness; the establishment of a free port ceased to be an important issue in the colony and was soon forgotten amid the repercussions of the American Revolution. Only Governor Hay kept the question before the Board of Trade in an occasional communication.[34]

It is interesting to note that the Barbadians seriously considered enacting a law on their own authority in an area clearly reserved for the sole jurisdiction of Parliament. Only the governor appears to have been in favor of promoting a free port by Parliamentary action. Had the proposed legislation been passed, and approved by the Board of Trade, it would have thrown open the entire realm of colonial commerce to the individual colonies and dealt a severe blow to the whole structure of empire.

In their haste to turn Parliamentary legislation to their own advantage the Barbadians had lost sight of the master plan so recently fashioned by the mother country for colonial control. Individual interests were to be subordinated to the empire as a whole; the selection of Jamaica and Dominica as free ports was not a bestowal of special favor on the two islands but rather part of a deliberate

[32] Governor Hay suggested to his Council on 3 August 1773 that Barbados ought to be made a free port by Parliament when the bill to renew the status of Dominica and Jamaica came before that body the following year. *C.O.* 31:34. See also 27 August 1773. *Idem*: Hay to Earl of Dartmouth, 24 August 1773. *C.O.* 28:55, no. 20.

[33] 31 August 1773. *C.O.* 31:36; 17 February 1774. *C.O.* 31:36; 14 October 1774. *C.O.* 31:39; 14 February 1774. *C.O.* 28:34, Hh. 11-12.

[34] Hay to Board of Trade, 2 June 1774. *C.O.* 29:21.

move to enhance the welfare of the entire commonwealth by sharing in the profits of French and Spanish West Indian commerce. As such, it marked the first step toward the eventual demise of the Acts of Trade in the nineteenth century, but in 1766, and for many years after, it could only be regarded as a device to augment their effectiveness.[35]

To argue that free trade throughout the empire would improve upon the existing system was to ignore the statistics of that trade. While the Acts were not without flaw, a remarkable structure of commerce and industry had been fostered and protected under their aegis, and a small island kingdom was able to gather riches far out of proportion to its own natural wealth and build upon those riches an economically integrated empire encompassing lands girdling the globe.

To contend, as did some Barbadians, that the British islands could successfully copy the Dutch trading pattern after the fashion of St. Eustatius was to misinterpret the basic strength of the empire which was grounded in the control of numerous products during all stages of their production, and not primarily upon the traders' profit inherent in the transfer of goods.[36] The Dutch had become specialists in the broker's role; for them it was the key to economic success. For the British to attempt the same would have dissipated the economic vitality of the empire upon the marketplace.

The free port debate was but another reflection of the desperation of the Barbadians over their continued loss of sufficiency in trade, and loss of status within the commonwealth. The localism in ideas and interests that had so long prevailed as the standard under which the islanders congregated in their dealings with the mother country

[35] It was generally accepted by writers of the period that the Jamaica free port was established primarily to supply British cotton and woolen manufacturers with their needed dyes and raw materials as cheaply as possible. Edwards states that "The quantities of these articles, as well as of woods for the dyer, imported in foreign bottoms into free-ports, are very considerable." "This subject was thoroughly investigated by the . . . Commons in 1774 (when the act would have expired); and it being in evidence that 30,000 people about Manchester were employed in the velvet manufactory, for which the San Domingo cotton and indigo had been imported from Jamaica at least thirty percent cheaper than the same could have been procured at through France – the House, disregarding all colonial opposition, came to a resolution, that the continuance of free-ports in Jamaica would be highly beneficial to the trade and manufactures of the kingdom. The act was thereupon renewed, and has since been made perpetual." (Edwards, *op. cit.*, p. 235).

[36] 17 February 1774. *C.O.* 31:36.

had by the seventh decade of the century ceased to serve as a successfull vehicle of communication. This was made still more unfortunate by the inability or unwillingness of Barbadian political leadership to recognize this fact.

V

THE AMERICAN YEARS

Lack of effective counter-measures to the Stamp Act by the Barbadians and the residents of other British islands had set the tone of future responses to the increased tempo of events on the North American mainland. More concerned with a renewed French threat, both economic and military, than with Parliamentary intrusions upon the rights of the various Assemblies, West Indian voices were seldom heard during the years immediately preceding 1775.

If sympathy for the American position existed, as it undoubtedly did, it was not manifest in the official dispatches of the period – either directly by government officials or by reports of dissatisfaction among the populace. This was to be expected however as official dispatches reflected official views, and every governor was anxious to maintain himself and his colony in the good graces of Whitehall and the Board of Trade. It was only when a rupture appeared imminent between Britain and her northern colonies that overtones of concern appear in the official correspondence – concern for the welfare of Barbados and not for the disaster which might befall fellow colonists to the north or the empire as a whole.

The papers of the period reflect a detachment from the affairs of empire that is often difficult to comprehend in view of the dependence of the Barbadians upon the smooth functioning of the colonial system. Perhaps it was anxiety over their own economic troubles that brought about this remoteness for the years following the Treaty of Paris were difficult indeed for the planters.

Sugar prices, though not as disastrously low as in 1763 and 1764, never rose from 38s. 3¼d. per hundredweight tending rather to average close to 36 s. for the nine year period from 1765 through 1773.[1]

[1] See Table II, pag. 34.

TABLE IV

Barbados exports in hundredweights: 1766-1784

	Sugar	Rum
1766	13,944	11,565–15,277
1767	8,512	10,710
1768	10,605	13,516
1769	11,903	10,687–15,435
1770	11,109	11,251–15,458
1771	6,314	9,148
1772	9,639	14,088
1773	—*	6,595
1775	—	3,353
1777	—	4,354
1778	—	2,058
1779	—	1,905
1780	—	2,527
1781	—	537
1782	—	559
1783	—	999
1784	—	3,315

* Exports from 1773-1784 are unavailable.
C.O. 31:34; *C.O.* 28:60, nos. 206-207.

Added to the misfortune of low prices was a series of poor harvests on Barbados first in 1768 and again from 1772 through 1775.[2]

Early dispatches after the removal of the disliked stamp tax reflect only calmness over the constitutional question and little uneasiness over the events in North America. Governor Spry reported to the Earl of Hillsborough late in 1768 (a poor year for the planters) that

[2] See Table IV. A memorial to the Board of Trade from the Barbados Assembly dated 14 February 1774, noted "The crops . . . have failed, from various causes, for a long series of years." *C.O.* 28:34. Hh. 11-12; Governor Hay stated "The state of trade is much the same as it has been for several years past, that is, rather in a decline owing to a series of bad crops. This year has hitherto been very dry." Hay to the Earl of Dartmouth, 31 August 1774. *C.O.* 28:55, nos 76-77. Southey states, "The crops of sugar in this year [1775] at Barbados were remarkably bad: thirty-one estates made only 6,400 pots of sugar of seventy pounds each. In a plentiful year one estate produces a larger quantity." Captain Thomas Southey, *Chronological History of the West Indies,* II (London, 1827), p. 422.

the island was "content", and that the government was proceeding "in a regular smooth settled course".[3] He took care to place himself and his government staunchly on the side of the established order by declaring a hope that any alterations in the

General Instructions, so as to effect a change in the present Constitution of the colony might not be attended with the same Public Utility in this island as perhaps it would in some of the North American governments.[4]

The following year Governor Spry reported that this Council and Assembly

concur in the Resolution of maintaining a due execution of the laws and in supporting the opinion of his majesty's servants that no measure ought to be taken which can any way derogate from the legislative authority of Great Britain over her colonies.[5]

Adding a personal word he further observed

The tenderness at the same time shown towards inhabitants of the colonies who have been greviously misled in North America by the arts of seditious, ill-denying persons, must prove a conciliating measure and it is to be hoped will soon bring on that tranquility and restore that affection in the colonies for the Mother Country on which the welfare and happiness of both so much depend. I have the satisfaction of commanding in a part of His Majesty's Dominions where Fraction and Sedition have not reared their heads. I find all ranks of persons here easy and satisfied with the blessings of peace which they enjoy.[6]

Here for the first time is official mention made of the interdependence of the colonies and the mother country, and an indication given of a grasp of the essential danger involved in the worsening relations between Britain and her northern colonies. But it is only mentioned – no more, for the remaining documents prior to 1775 merely contain references to items of a parochial nature, and continued declarations of loyalty.[7]

The chief cause of concern over the growing rift on the mainland was its probable effect upon the Barbados economy. Again we note a persistence in pleading the issue solely in terms of the welfare of

[3] Spry to the Earl of Hillsborough, 24 September 1768. *C.O.* 28:33, Gg. 20.
[4] *Idem.*
[5] Spry to the Earl of Hillsborough, 8 July 1769. *C.O.* 28:33, Gg. 34.
[6] *Idem.*
[7] Spry to Hillsborough, 1 December 1769. Assures him of the affection of Barbados for the king. *C.O.* 28:33, duplicate no. 26; Spry to Hillsborough, 9 March 1770. Notes that Barbados is tranquil in contrast to "some other parts of His Majesty's dominions." *C.O.* 28:33, duplicate no. 28.

Barbados, minus any attempt to assume leadership in a movement toward a solution of the question which so vitally affected all the British West Indies. For the colony which had for so many years claimed dominance in West Indian thought based upon its recognized position as the "mother-colony" in the Caribbean, this alone accurately portrays the extent of its decline.

While the hard facts of economic life were to eventually drive all interested parties within the empire to the same position with regard to the North American problem, this does not and should not be allowed to stand as an excuse for political inaction both in thought and deed. Certainly if there was a valid reason for inaction, the paralysis of political perception from which the Barbadians suffered for so many years offered them a sound pardon.

It is easier and more reasonable however to look to Britain for our answer. The inability of the Barbadians or any of the other planter groups to play an important healing role can be traced to the same set of circumstances surrounding the breakdown of communication in America. Despite the confusion of British politics after 1763, an unyielding attitude toward the colonies was exhibited: they must be kept in economic subordination to those powerful interests which profited from colonial commerce and investments overseas.[8] Individual colonies might still receive affirmative responses from the Board of Trade on requests for projects of a local nature (e.g. free ports), but only if such moves would further the cause of mercantilism so as to benefit the many.

The suggestions put forward by the West Indians usually failed to penetrate to the basic core of the difficulty, and thus, fell wide of the mark in attempting to find a solution to the growing dispute in North America. It is probable though that barring a complete reversal in British economic policy little could have been done to alter the flow of events after 1769 regardless of the political astuteness of the planters. There was no shortage of spokesmen in England, or in Parliament itself, to remind the ministers of George III of the grave risks being undertaken in the name of mercantilism; it is hard to imagine that colonial voices – even the most politically discerning, could hope to be more persuasive.

Concern with events in North America tended to vary directly with

[8] Sir Lewis Naimer's *The Structure of Politics at the Accession of George III* (London, 1929), and *England in the Age of the American Revolution* (London, 1930), are excellent references on British political thought.

the assumed threat to the welfare of Barbados. Since the threat was considered primarily to be of an economic nature, and since the Barbadians had for years maintained close ties with the merchants of the leading American cities, any action that would tend to jeopardize those ties was viewed with alarm. Boycotts of British goods, riots, destruction of property, and counter-measures in general by the Americans to the edicts of Parliament and the Board of Trade annoyed the planters far more than the original enactments themselves.

Fear of endangering the economic status quo caused many Barbadians to suppress their private sympathies in favor of expressions of dismay over the effrontery of the Americans. The most commonly used approach was that of placing the responsibility for events on the evil intent of a few rabblerousers and the credulousness of the population. A memorial to Governor Spry from the Assembly written during the crisis created by American reaction to the Townsend duties in 1769 asserted

> Involved as the inhabitants of this, as well as all the other islands necessarily are in the consequences [of the North American disturbances], we cannot but lament the cause of those jealousies which have for sometime past disturbed the minds of our fellow subjects upon the Northern Continent, nor look with less impatience than themselves for the result of those more tender and deliberate counsels which shall restore America to its former general quiet by placing it, as formerly, in the full esteem and kindness of the Parent Country.[9]

By the summer of 1774 events in North America threatened to disrupt the entire pattern of colonial commerce. Incensed by the destruction of £15,000 worth of East India Company tea by a band of American radicals disguised as Indians, Parliament had passed the Boston Port Bill which removed the customhouse from Boston and closed the port to all shipping until such time as restitution was made to the company for its tea. This was certain to be disruptive of Barbados business – long dependent upon Boston as an outlet for much of its sugar, rum, and molasses, and as the source of many of the commodities necessary for the maintenance of life on the island.

Compounding the already serious situation was the probability of additional American action in retaliation against the Port Bill. The Barbadians were convinced that the Americans would once again resort to the use of economic weapons, probably an embargo of British goods, in their attempt to counter this latest Parliamentary move. The

[9] Barbados Assembly to Governor Spry, 14 March 1769. *C.O.* 31:35.

Assembly expressed the foreboding that must have been widely felt on Barbados; in a message to Governor Hay it stated

We reflect with a pleasure equal to that expressed by Your Excellency on the present disposition of the inhabitants of this island; we reflect upon this temper and good agreement amongst our countrymen as a mark of their prudence no less than their virtue at so critical a juncture as the present, when they must be waiting with a fearful expectation of the event of those troubles in which our brethren upon the northern continent of America are unhappily involved with our mother country, and in which from that natural connection and dependence of the distant settlements on each other, the people of these Southern Colonies must soon find themselves deeply interested and affected.[10]

Only a week before the Continental Congress assembled in Philadelphia to decide upon a plan of resistance to the authority of Parliament, Governor Hay reported to the Board of Trade that

Some people have been apprehensive of the North Americans shutting up their ports, and witholding their provision and lumber; hitherto as many as usual have come here from North America. For my part I am more apprehensive of the effects of a dry year, than of any distress from the North Americans.[11]

Acting to offset the general fear of privation which would result from a break in commercial relations with the northern colonies was the belief that even if the Continental Congress were to declare an embargo, enforcement would be difficult because of the number of Americans vitally interested in the West India trade.[12] The question was soon to be settled, for on 20 October 1774, the Congress declared that unless its demands for autonomy within the empire were met the ports of America would be closed to most British Caribbean produce after 1 December 1774, and a complete trade embargo would take effect after 10 September 1775.

News of the proclamation arrived in the Antilles with the first ships out of Philadelphia. The embargo, if successfully instituted, would strike at the very heart of West Indian sufficiency and pose a grave threat to British supremacy in the Caribbean. This fact was not lost upon the Barbados merchants and planters who composed a sizeable majority in the Assembly, but it remained for the Jamaican Assembly

[10] Barbados Assembly to Governor Hay, 19 July 1774. *C.O.* 31:34.

[11] Hay to the Earl of Dartmouth, 31 August 1774. *C.O.* 28:55, nos. 76-77.

[12] Governor Payne of the Leeward Islands to the Earl of Dartmouth, 3 July 1774, as quoted in Ragatz, *op. cit.*, p. 142.

to champion colonial rights in general and approach the Crown on behalf of the North Americans.[13]

In a strongly worded petition to the king passed in the closing hours of its session, the Assembly professed its loyalty but declared that destruction of the sugar trade "must follow the unnatural contest with the Americans".[14] The petitioners asserted further that the colonists were not subject to the laws of England, apart from those regulating external commerce, and insisted that all others were the sole prerogative of local legislatures. This was a firm denial of the right of Parliament to legislate beyond selected areas of broad colonial policy and to interfere in the internal affairs of the colonies. Following the pattern used by American petitioners of the period the Assembly appealed to the king to "become a mediator between his European and American subjects", so "that no laws shall be forced upon them injurious to their rights as colonists or Englishmen . . ."[15]

The memorial was foredoomed to failure. The Earl of Dartmouth attacked the "so indecent, not to say criminal conduct of the Assembly" and threatened the perpetrators of the document with punishment if they failed to reconsider their ill-timed action.[16] The legislature of Connecticut and the Continental Congress on the other hand extended votes of thanks to the Jamaicans for their efforts in the cause of peace.[17]

The quickening pace of events in North America was watched with growing alarm by the membership of the West India Merchants in England. As any disruption in the colonial trade pattern would adversely affect the marketing of sugar, the group stood ready to bring its influence to bear wherever and whenever it seemed most appropriate. Late in 1773 the Merchants considered a motion to ask Parliament to permit "all kinds of corn and grain (except wheat) and also biscuit to be exported to the sugar colonies without limitation . . ." to create a reserve supply of provisions in the event of war.[18]

The decision of the Continental Congress to suspend all commerce in the thirteen colonies backed by the treat of force against dissenters,

[13] *Idem.*

[14] "Memorial from the General Assembly of Jamaica Relative to the Present State of American Affairs to His Majesty George III", 14 December 1774, as quoted in Southey, *op. cit.*, pp. 422-423.

[15] *Idem.*

[16] Dartmouth to Governor Keith of Jamaica, 3 March 1775. *C.O.* 137:70.

[17] Ragatz, *op. cit.*, p. 143.

[18] Minutes of the West India Merchants, First Series, I, 7 December 1773.

occasioned the calling of a general meeting open to all persons having an interest in the West Indies "... to deliberate on the steps necessary to be taken by us jointly on the present important crisis."[19] The meeting was held 18 January 1775, at the London Tavern, Bishopsgate Street and a petition prepared for transmission to Parliament.

It was the desire of the group to make its fears known to Parliament in as strong a manner as possible, and to secure from the lawmakers some assurance that West Indian interests would receive the full protection and support of the government for the duration of the crisis. The document set forth the apprehension felt over the impending American boycott and suggested that Parliament take concerted action to placate the northern colonists for the sake of the British investment in the Caribbean valued at £30,000,000. It suggested also that without "free" access to North American provisions the islands would certainly suffer extreme privation which would endanger their safety and adversely affect national revenues. The petitioners noted

> That the profits arising from the present state of the said islands, and that are likely to arise from their future improvement, in a great measure depend on a free and reciprocal intercourse between them and the several provinces of North America.[20]

In the Commons the matter was referred to a committee to hear evidence in support of the petition. In the House of Lords the memorial became submerged for several weeks in a personal feud between the Marquis of Rockingham and the Earl of Dartmouth over a point of order unrelated to the question at hand and was soundly rejected when finally brought to a vote late in March. The opening of hostilities soon after brought an end to all attempts at settlement through West Indian intervention.[21]

In April Governor Hay reported the "storehouses ... well stocked" on Barbados, and that trade with North America continued to flourish in spite of the Congressional edict and a small sugar crop occasioned by drought. On the eve of war in North America his letter seems inept and unrealistic; especially is this true in light of the strenuous effort on behalf of compromise and reconciliation taken by the West India Committee. Hay stated

> It is the sincere wish of every faithful subject that his Majesty's steady

[19] *Ibid.*, 3 January 1775.
[20] *Ibid.*, 7 February 1775.
[21] Ragatz, *op. cit.*, p. 144.

Resolution to maintain the authority of the supreme legislature over all His Majesty's Dominions, thus supported by his Parliament, may have the desired effect upon the minds of his subjects in America. It is with pleasure I acquaint your Lordship, that no bad effect has been felt in this island hitherto from the disturbances in the northern colonies, but that full as many vessels with provisions and stores have arrived from thence as usual and the storehouses are well stocked. Therefore as we may justly hope that those people will return to a proper sense of their duty, so I think there is little to fear from any ill-consequence to this island henceforward.[22]

Only four days before the battle of Lexington, Parliament acted to restrict the commerce of Massachusetts, New Hampshire, Connecticut, and Rhode Island by formally closing their trade with the British West Indies. In a series of acts taking effect on 1 July 1775, elaborate precautions were instituted to halt the flow of provisions and supplies southward to the Caribbean.[23] The immediate result was to increase the number of prize ships brought to Barbados and thus the supply of provisions on the island.

At such a critical juncture the increased flow of food and plantation stores was of vital importance. Although in no actual danger of invasion by American forces, the islands would soon be faced by the very real threat of privation resulting from a lack of supplies unless a substitute source could be artifically established. Governor Hay continued to report the island in satisfactory condition. The Earl of Dartmouth noted with pleasure "that the disturbances in the Northern Colonies have not yet had any effect to prevent the island of Barbados from being supplied with those articles that have usually been imported from thence".[24] However the foremost nineteenth-century authority on the West Indies, R.H. Schomburgk, states

Instead of providing for such an emergency by legislative means, the time was allowed to pass until the rupture actually took place, when to their great consternation the Barbaians found that their stock of provisions was estimated at scarcely six weeks consumption.[25]

The precise condition of Barbados and the other British islands is clouded by numerous conflicting documents on the subject. Governor Hay had been embroiled in controversy with his Assembly since his

[22] Hay to Dartmouth, 6 April 1775. *C.O.* 28:56, nos. 1-3; *C.O.* 29:21.

[23] 15 George III. c. 10, acts 34-39. The act was extended in May 1775, to include New Jersey, Pennsylvania, Maryland, Virginia, and South Carolina. 15 George III c. 18.

[24] Dartmouth to Hay, 5 July 1775. *C.O.* 28:56, no. 6.

[25] R. H. Schomburgk, *The History of Barbados* (London, 1848), p. 333.

arrival in 1773 and was not apt to acknowledge in writing any distress on the island regardless of the circumstances or causes. An obstinate and self-centered official with little knowledge of colonial affairs and still less of the Barbadian viewpoint, he had lost touch with the mood of his citizens by the outbreak of the American Revolution.[26] In the Assembly several individuals fearful for their own interests in time of war took every opportunity to voice their concern over the events in distorted terms, stimulated by the desire to embarrass the governor before his superiors in London. Statements regarding the condition of Barbados were often designed as tools for use in the internal power struggle, and as such are suspect for any purpose beyond that of showing the intensity of the conflict over prerogatives waged between Governor Hay and his Assembly.

By late summer the Governor had become alternately optimistic and pessimistic in his dispatches to the Board of Trade. While declaring that the "Disturbances in North America have not hitherto affected this island", and that provisions were in such great supply "that for many years they had not been known to be so cheap as in May last", Hay acknowledged that he had forbidden the export of foodstuffs "as long as the island is threatened to have provisions withheld".[27] He noted further that several cargoes of provisions had arrived since July, but that he was not expecting "much more unless from those colonies who have not sent deputies to the Congress", although he reiterated his belief that regardless of the congressional edict most North American traders would still do "what is most for their own interest".[28]

As a hedge against a food shortage many of the planters began to cultivate large crops of Indian and Guinea corn on portions of their sugar lands. The corn and other ground crops would do much to make many estates self-sufficient during the lean years ahead. Coupled with adequate provisions in storage and the arrival of numerous prizes during the first few months of the Revolution, Barbados appears to have weathered the initial shock of the disruption of her trade.

[26] See Ragatz, *op. cit.*, p. 151.

[27] Hay to Dartmouth, 29 August 1775. *C.O.* 28:56, nos. 10-12.

[28] *Idem.* Another version of this communication reads: "We are not apprehensive of any bad effect from the conduct of North America. Indeed I am inclined to believe whatever may be the public declaration of their General Congress, individuals after a certain time will be apt to do what is most for their own interests." Hay to Dartmouth, 29 August 1775. *C.O.* 29:21.

Even nature was kind to the planters by providing an abundant harvest after a succession of poor years.[29]

The abundance of provisions proved to be only temporary however, and within a year the supply had dwindled sufficiently to cause concern among the planters. A food shortage could easily set off the most feared of all occurrences – a slave rebellion. Only the strictest of measures had spared the planters such an event in the past, and only by constant surveillance was the established order maintained at all. The prospect of sixty thousand starving slaves staging a mass uprising in an attempt to secure food was almost too frightful to contemplate. A steady flow of provisions therefore was, and would be, necessary to preserve the precarious balance of order and tranquility upon which the welfare of all depended.

In February, 1776, the Assembly made a direct appeal to the king for relief from the approaching "famine" which they felt would soon appear barring direct aid from England.[30] The motion to petition had been introduced by the island's Solicitor-General, Henry Duke, an antagonist of Governor Hay from the beginning of the latter's term, and a strong advocate of Assembly freedom. Hay seized the opportunity to remove Duke from his position, and wrote of him in a letter to the Board as a man "who ought to have had other sentiments than those of disturbing the king's peace of mind at so critical a jucture".[31]

The Governor's unfavorable reaction to the petition appears to have been based more upon his personal dislike of Solicitor-General Duke and the affronty of his Assembly in daring to address the king directly than upon a firm conviction that its contents were in error. Only two days previous to his letter of the fifteenth Hay had written Lord Germaine that the corn had not done as well as expected and since trade with North America had been cut off by Parliament "the planters begin to apprehend a scarcity of many articles necessary for their plantations".[32]

The situation was further complicated by the arrival of several British ships from Boston with orders from General Sir William Howe

[29] Hay to John Pownall, 29 August 1775. *C.O.* 28:56, no. 22.

[30] Barbados Assembly to George III, 11 February 1776. *C.O.* 28:56, nos. 33-36. The petitioners claimed that the Barbados population contained 80,000 Negroes and 20,000 whites. This estimate is probably too high – deliberately so, to add emphasis to the plea. More reliable population estimates give the figure of approximately 65,000 slaves and 15,000 whites.

[31] Hay to Lord George Germaine, 15 February 1776. *C.O.* 28:56, nos. 29-30.

[32] Hay to Germaine, 13 February 1776. *C.O.* 28:56, nos. 26-28.

to acquire rum, beef, and pork for his troops surrounded in the city. The requested food was supplied in spite of "the scarcity of provisions . . ." on the island and the general temper of the populace.[33]

The petition was presented to Lord Germaine by George Walker, the Barbados agent in Londen, who accompanied it with a memorial of his own describing the depressed state of affairs on the island. Germaine replied that since the conditions claimed to exist in both the petition and memorial were contrary to reports received in the dispatches of Governor Hay nothing would be done for the present.[34]

When news of the petition's failure reached the Assembly several resolutions were passed affirming that body's right to address the throne, and condemning Governor Hay for interfering in the attempt to secure a measure of relief for the colony. Led again by Mr. Duke a second petition was voted.[35] This declared that the Governor was deliberately thwarting all efforts to supply the island with much-needed provisions, and that by so doing he was endangering the welfare of Barbados merely to satisfy his own vanity. It also stated that poor whites and Negroes were "suffering" for lack of food, prices were continuing to rise, and "large quantities" of rum were "remaining unsold" for lack of a market.[36]

Although publicly declaring the adequacy of provisions on Barbados the Governor was privately casting about for an informal method of ending the drain upon the colony's already scanty reserve of food. In a letter to Vice Admiral Young, commander of the British fleet in the Antilles, Hay suggested allowing Barbados ships to trade directly with the French and Dutch islands, and the sending of all ships carrying North American produce to Barbados, "where they will meet with a very good price for all their articles".[37] He concluded the message with the admission that "this island is in great distress for want of support for their Negroes, and which distress is likely to increase daily as long as this unhappy contest between the Mother Country and the North American Colonies subsists".[38]

The admiral replied favorably to the suggestion, but expressed fear that private importation of provisions from the French and Dutch islands might enrich a few individuals, or "secure from capture the

[33] *Idem.*
[34] Ragatz, *op. cit.*, p. 151.
[35] *Idem.*; Minutes of the Barbados Assembly, 7 July 1776. *C.O.* 31:39.
[36] Barbados Assembly to George III, 9 July 1776. *C.O.* 28:56, nos. 70-72.
[37] Hay to Vice Admiral Young, 24 March 1776. *C.O.* 28:56, nos. 51-52.
[38] *Idem.*

property of the North American rebels and afterwards only become a monopoly in the hands of their friends (the disaffected people in the different islands) which is certainly an advantage they are in no wise entitled to".[39] To prevent possible abuse, the admiral proposed the establishment of a public corporation vested with the sole right to carry on such a trade; immediate relief could be obtained by purchasing captured American provisions at Antigua.[40] The Barbados Council approved the project and suggested raising the necessary capital by sale of stock. Lack of subscriptions, however, caused the idea to collapse within a few weeks.[41]

By the spring of 1776 the general uncertainty surrounding the continued supply of provisions, even in limited quantities, coupled with a marked increase in insurance and shipping rates, had forced food prices noticeably upward throughout the Caribbean. On Barbados Governor Hay had become a victim of his own emotions. While continuing to report an abundance of provisions on the island in his dispatches to London, the governor felt obliged to criticize the colony's merchants whom he blamed for raising prices on most items considered as staples, and therefore necessary to the well-being of the populace.

In April Hay reported a need for "India and Guinea corn for the Negroes", while noting that livestock was plentiful and that there was no shortage of provisions originating in England and Ireland. He complained that "the traders" were keeping prices up, but then contradicted himself in an attack upon his enemies in the Assembly who

> talk of Famine, in the most plentiful Island of all the West Indies, and where I, who have no plantation and must buy all the provisions for my Table, can assure your Lordship that scarcely One Article of provisions and live Stock of the Island has varied in price for near these three Years that I have been here.[42]

Three months later the Governor again censured the "storekeepers" for their "high prices", but noted several vessels containing provisions "that have called here have gone away for want of purchasers".[43]

[39] Vice Admiral Young to Hay, Antigua, 2 April 1776. *C.O.* 28:56, nos. 53-54.

[40] *Idem.* The Barbados Council also proposed direct trade with the French, Dutch, and Spanish islands. *C.O.* 29:21.

[41] Ragatz, *op. cit.*, p. 152; Hay to Germaine, 25 July 1776. *C.O.* 28:56, nos. 61-63; *C.O.* 29:21.

[42] Hay to Germaine, 13 April 1776. *C.O.* 28:56, nos. 40-41.

[43] Hay to Germaine, 25 July 1776. *C.O.* 28:56, nos. 61-63; *C.O.* 29:21.

The situation might have been far worse in the colony if the Admiralty in February 1776, acting upon the urging of both Parliament and several influential planters on the West India Committee, had not agreed to convoy merchant shipping to and from Great Britain and the Caribbean.[44] In an address before his Council and Assembly at the opening of the new session Hay took notice of the convoys and of a more recent act of Parliament authorizing the direct exportation of wheat and other grains from Great Britain to the West Indies.[45] In one of his few conciliatory speeches before the legislators Hay remarked upon the hardships then being faced by all, and noted that they

> must feel the effects of a suspension of trade with so many of His Majesty's Northern Colonies in America as are now in rebellion; nor was it possible that His West India islands could be exempt from a large share of inconvenience from this interruption.[46]

However, "the provident care of His Majesty and both houses of Parliament", he felt, would soon rectify those past hardships, and the Americans would probably surrender before the end of the year anyhow.[47]

The Council assumed a mild tone in replying to the Governor's message, but took note of the basic problem facing the colony – that of the loss of its primary market for sugar.

> Not to feel the calamities which surround us, not to deprecate the evils arising from the unnatural conditions on the continent would argue a deficiency of every sentiment which humanity as well as self-preservation could suggest. Yet confident of the wisdom of His Majesty's councils and firmly attached to his person and government, we look with patience and resignation for a happy period [conclusion] of contests that have been so extensive and unsparing in their effects, so very prejudicial to us. Your excellency views with just complacency the successive and unexpected supplies by which we have been relieved from threatened distress. But [this cannot] give contentment to the industrious planter beyond the exigencies of the present hour. The surplus of our produce yields but little advantage, when the accustomed markets for our staple commodities are shut against us. With decent aquiescence however we must bear misfortunes which originate not among ourselves – trusting that oppression will cease to guide the hand

[44] Minutes of the West India Merchants, First Series, I, 16 February 1776.

[45] Hay to Barbados Council and Assembly, 22 August 1776. *C.O.* 31:34. The exportation was authorized by 16 George III c. 37, and subsequently renewed annually for the duration.

[46] *Idem.*

[47] *Idem; C.O.* 28:56, no. 84.

of the importunate creditor and that every measure will be adopted which can alleviate these surrounding evils.[48]

The Assembly used the occasion to assail Hay for his ineptitude in office and his continuing failure to agree with the Assembly members as to the seriousness of the situation confronting the colony. Parliament was censured for prohibiting Barbados trade with North America while failing to open a substitute channel. While the island was to receive wheat from Britain to ease the food shortage, none had yet arrived, prices were rising and the poor white people, according to the Assembly, were "starving".[49] Hay was bitterly attacked for allowing food to be sent to General Howe the previous spring in spite of the serious shortage and the uncertainty of supply.[50]

Early in the session the Assembly sent still another petition to the king. It was still too soon to have received a reply from their second memorial written in July, but the prospect of a mediocre crop of corn galvanized the planters into action. The petitioners asserted that Barbados could not hope to become self-sufficient in food and claimed a shortage of grain "more especially in those parts of the island that have always depended upon the grain of North America for their subsistence to keep their slaves from perishing".[51] Large quatities of rum allegedly remained unsold for lack of a suitable market, since the former trade with North America had been "cut off" by legislative fiat.[52]

In London, Agent Walker had laid the Assembly's second petition before the king, and had also composed a memorial of his own which he presented to Lord Germaine. In it he noted the sharp rise in food prices in the colony since the start of the American Revolution and the equally distressing fall in sugar prices paid to the planters. Walker claimed that sugar was selling for twenty-six to forty percent less than it had only two years earlier, and that "the poor white people are on the point of perishing in most parts of the island . . ." for want of sustenance.[53] Negroes were reportedly stealing cattle from the fields and slaughtering them immediately for food, while private

[48] Barbados Council to Governor Hay, 1 October 1776. *C.O.* 31:34.

[49] Barbados Assembly to Governor Hay, 1-2 October 1776. *C.O.* 28:56, nos. 88-91; *C.O.* 31:34.

[50] *Idem.*

[51] Barbados Assembly to George III, 9 September 1776. *C.O.* 29:21.

[52] *Idem.*

[53] George Walker to Lord Germaine, Cavandish Square, London, 9 and 11 September 1776. *C.O.* 28:56; nos. 75-76; *C.O.* 31:39.

cornfields were being robbed by desperate bands of starving people. The memorial also asserted that many of the Barbadians were fleeing out of desperation and fear to the French held island of St. Lucia, and that many others might easily be persuaded to transfer their loyalty if they did not soon receive aid! The distress on Barbados was compared with that of Lisbon after the great earthquake and fire in 1755 when sixty thousand people perished.

Walker included a table of commodity prices for Barbados in his memorial representing the period 1774–75, and the year 1776. By the use of this device he was able to show a one hundred fifty percent rise in basic food prices in less than twenty-four months and a four hundred percent increase in the price of corn alone!

Commodity	*1774–1775*	*1776*
Good Flour from	15s. to 25s. per container	*Bad* flour 30s. to 37s. 6d.
Ship corn (maize)	2s. 6d. to 3s. 9d. per bu.	10s. to 13s.
Salt fish	12s. 6d. to 25s. per quintat	30s. to 40s.
Beef	60s. to 70s. per barrel	90s. to 130s.
Pork	70s. to 100s. per barrel	100s. to 150s.
Herrings	25s. to 32s. 6d. per barrel	45s. to 55s.
Butter	8d. to 10d. per pound	1s. 3d. to 1s. 10½d.
Muscovado	30s. to 35s. per hwt.	18s. 9d. to 25s.
Rum	2s. per gallon	1s. 3d.[54]

The second petition and Agent Walker's memorial became lost in the machinery of government procedure after the fashion of countless others. Indeed, it was doubtful whether the mother country could do more than was already being done on behalf of the British West Indies: a naval force of considerable strength was on station in the Caribbean, merchant shipping was convoyed in both directions between England and the British islands, wheat had been sent out in large quantity from Britain to relieve a food shortage, and the Barbadians were allowed to carry on direct importation of provisions from the foreign islands.

The basic hardship caused by the war – loss of the primary market for Barbados sugar and rum, could not be remedied by king or Par-

[54] *Idem.*

liament. Regardless of the inroads made by the cheaper French sugars, North America continued to be the greatest single importer of Barbados sugar up to the eve of the Revolution. The American market had expanded so rapidly from 1764 on that even the relatively high priced Barbados sugar had found an outlet. With the harbors of the mainland closed to them the Barbados planters faced ruin more total and complete than if the war itself had come to their lands.

In pleading for relief from "starvation" the planters were pleading not only for their physical well-being, but for their economic life as well. We may hypothesize that the incessant pleas by the Assembly for aid to relieve the physical miseries of the populace were but a mask behind which to hide the true crisis facing the colony, or we may assume that the petitions were a sincere attempt to act in the public interest and that only a question of emphasis remained for debate. The actions of Governor Hay and the Assembly support both assumptions. The Governor, for all his obtuseness, appears to have divined the true condition of his colony far more accurately than his antagonists in the Assembly, as there is no documentary proof, beyond a rise in prices, to substantiate the claims of either the Assembly or the Barbados Agent, George Walker.

The Assembly's persistence in pleading for relief after September 1776 suggests an insincerity bordering upon the whimsical, for supplies and foodstuffs were reaching the island in good order and the colony was in little danger of famine from that time on to the end of the war. However, the crises engendered by war had always brought to the surface the fears of privation and danger which continually lurked somewhere in the consciousness of every citizen. These anxieties would, by the nature of government, find expression in the Assembly. Pleas for additional food were a communication of those fears, but exaggerated during this particular conflict by the nature of the circumstances. For the first time in the one hundred fifty year history of Barbados war had brought with it the threat of absolute economic destruction through the loss of the colony's primary arteries of trade.

The realization of this danger by the Assembly early in 1776 appears to have been responsible for the rash of words concerning the plight of the colony. Governor Hay, who had seen through the distortion of the Assembly's claims was nonetheless unable to perceive the basic concern which motivated those gentlemen, and this failure effectively ruled out the Governor as an agent for the cause of moderation. Actually Hay had established himself in opposition to his lower house long before the current crisis, and it is doubtful whether the Governor would have been able to exert much influence under those conditions regardless of his powers of perception. This antagonism only served to lessen the effectiveness of both the Governor and the planter interests.

Other than occasional references to the need for provisions of an undefined nature, and not necessarily food, the question of "starvation" and "famine" ceased to be of official importance after 1776. It had become obvious that all that could be done to lessen the threat of privation was already being done by the mother country.[55] The official attitude toward the problem was expressed by Lord Germaine who stated that he would rather believe Governor Hay than the Barbados Assembly concerning the situation and that he was personally satisfied that the colony was in no immediate danger of famine and would remain secure by the continuing efforts of the home government.[56]

As the American war progressed into 1777 the tone of the official papers becomes more somber. Although the general condition of Barbados remained sound, occasional crises did develop in the supply situation caused by delays in shipping or by partial failures in the local food crop. The Assembly continued to resort to the use of the aid petition during these periods, and unlike those of previous years these latter requests were often hastily fulfilled. Upon receipt of such a petition in October of 1777 the Government sent out a supply of additional provisions consisting of beef, pork, flour at 25s. per bushel, beans at 5s. and peas at 10s. per bushel.[57]

Early in the conflict there had been talk of an American invasion of several British islands. It was never seriously contemplated however, though a group of American seamen managed to capture Nas-

[55] Governor Hay wrote late in 1777, "foreign provisions are very scarce for the want of the arrival of a convoy from England and Ireland", and again in 1779 that provisions were in short supply. Hay to Germaine, 24 October 1777 and 5 April 1779. *C.O.* 28:57, nos. 1-2; *C.O.* 28:57, nos. 84-86. Hay also suggested that if the planters continued to plant corn on Barbados they would not have to import so much from North America after the war, and thus save money. Hay to Germaine, 7 December 1776. *C.O.* 28:56, nos. 96-98.

[56] Germaine to Hay, 2 October 1776. *C.O.* 28:56, nos. 77-78. Germaine did express his pleasure upon learning that a supply convoy had arrived in Barbados in the spring of 1778 "... to relieve the distresses of the inhabitants and their slaves which appear to have been much greater than there was reason to apprehend." Germaine to Hay, 3 June 1778. *C.O.* 28:57, nos. 21-22.

[57] Whitehall, 25 October 1777. *C.O.* 31:34. A shipment of herrings sent in relief in February 1778 was sold at 30s. a barrel. *C.O.* 31:34.

sau, capital of the Bahamas, for a few days at the outset of the Revolution. The foolhardy proposals of Silas Deane to incite the slaves of Jamaica and the Caribs of St. Vincent to rebel against the British were also barren of results.[58] The presence of American privateers in the Caribbean posed an entirely different threat to the British colonies throughout the war. Ranging widely throughout the Indies scores of American raiders were able to maintain a constant pressure upon a large portion of the Royal Navy and tie down several dozen British warships which might have been used elsewhere. West Indian shipping was in continuous danger of destruction or capture and even the use of convoys offered no protection to the countless coastal craft which plied among the various islands.

Almost from the outbreak of the Revolution American ships had found refuge and welcome at Guadeloupe and Martinique. After Congress opened commercial relations between the rebelling colonies and the foreign West Indies in October 1775, both the large French islands became centers of American operations in the Antilles. Relations between the British and French colonists became badly strained over the French acceptance of the Americans in their harbors and over the French refusal to prohibit the disposal of prize ships and cargoes by the privateers. Governor Hay complained that "the French Governor at Martinique . . . suffers the American vessels to come into his ports with their prizes; many American cruisers have been fitted out at Martinique, and chiefly manned with Frenchmen and other foreigners . . . We have several Americans on this coast. Captain Helme with a cargo from London was taken off this island."[59]

The appointment of a new governor for Martinique in the spring of 1777 gave Governor Hay hope that the appointment might presage a change in French policy concerning the Americans and that Barbados might soon be rid of the raiders now harbored only one hundred twenty miles away. Noting that the number of American privateers had "lessened these past few months", Hay expressed the belief "that the new Governor General of the French islands, the Comte de Bouille, gives no encouragement to the Americans, which was not the case with his predecessor".[60]

[58] Ragatz, *op. cit.*, p. 145. Governor Hay however requested the Admiralty late in 1776 to send additional warships into the area to "prevent an American attack upon us". Hay to Germaine, 12 October 1776. *C.O.* 28:56, nos. 79-82.

[59] Hay to Germaine, 25 February 1777. *C.O.* 28:56, nos. 105-106.

[60] Hay to Germaine, 3 June, 1777. *C.O.* 28:56, nos. 115-116.

Hay's optimism was of short duration. In response to an inquiry, de Bouille replied that the English and Americans were all English to him and that since France and England were at peace he could not close his harbors to any subject of the British Crown and would therefore treat them equally![61] Thus American captains continued to find protection in the French island for themselves and their prizes. French assistance had become so blatant by 1777 that when a British man-of-war forced the capture of an American privateer a count of the crew revealed the presence of forty-nine French and only one American on board.[62]

The continued American attacks so infuriated Hay that he wrote the French Governor a series of notes demanding expulsion of the Americans from Martinique and Guadeloupe and the return of captured Barbados property. Hay implied that failure to act might lead to a rupture between the two countries.[63] In July the Assembly voted funds for the support of a small ship which sailed around the island in an effort to protect coastal shipping, and the Governor sought permission to equip two additional ships for the same purpose.[64] The effectiveness of these ships was questionable, as the Americans continued to infest Barbados waters. In August Hay complained that the Americans still came to Barbados on "small French vessels" to spy on the island without anchoring,[65] and two months later a private citizen wrote, "The privateers belonging to the provincials have made several captures of vessels bound from hence to England and many loyal inhabitants of the West Indies have suffered much by the war . . ."[66]

In October the Admiralty granted colonial governors permission to issue letters of marque "upon the application of the owners of trading vessels fitted out" in the British islands.[67] The Governor, fearing to create additional furor which might incite the French to still greater excesses, and fearing the improper use of the letters in the hands of

[61] Hay to Germaine, 12 July 1777. *C.O.* 28:56, nos. 126-128.

[62] *Idem.*

[63] Hay to Governor General de Bouille, 14-15 June 1777. *C.O.* 28:56, nos. 129-131. In the letter Hay reported that an American schooner had stolen thirty or forty Negroes and several fishing boats from the northern part of Barbados, and that he wished de Bouille to get them back.

[64] Hay to Germaine, 17 July 1777. *C.O.* 28:56, nos. 137-138; *C.O.* 29:21.

[65] Hay to de Bouille, 13 August 1777. *C.O.* 28:57, nos. 5-7.

[66] The Attorney for Codrington College to the Reverend Dr. Hind, Secretary to the S.P.G., London, 7 October 1777.

[67] Hay to Germaine, 24 October 1777. *C.O.* 28:57, nos. 1-2.

the "lower sort of people", was reluctant to use his authority.[68] Hay stated his intention to use caution in the issuance of the commissions and declared "I have no great opinion of many of the traders and seafaring people of the West Indies."[69]

There was good reason for the Governor to suspect the motives, and perhaps the loyalty, of many of the local merchants, for many of them were willing to place their own welfare above that of the colony and their fellow traders. For many the war was regarded more as an economic evil than as a political misfortune and the outcome was viewed with indifference. Smuggling had long been rife in the Indies and in time of war it became an economic necessity for many. On Barbados there were numerous merchants with whom illegal trading activities had become an established pattern, even at the risk of dealing with the Americans.

Although corresponding or trading with the enemy in wartime was not considered a treasonable act in the eighteenth century, it was prohibited by statute and punishable by fine and imprisonment throughout most of the British empire. During the American Revolution the Barbados Assembly did renew an act passed in 1757 prohibiting His Majesty's subjects on Barbados from corresponding with those of "the king's enemies, and from supplying them with provisions or warlike stores of any kind".[70] It is significant however that the Assembly delayed taking action until four years after the start of the Revolution and took action then only after the entry of France in the war. As there were sizeable groups of merchants in the Assembly we may assume that they did not act against their best interests and were in a position to block Assembly action which they viewed as prejudicial to those interests. War with France always presented a real danger to Barbados. To aid the French would be to jeopardize the safety of the colony in the face of possible invasion or siege; to aid the American cause in the course of trade would be incidental to the benefit accruing to Barbados by the importation of badly needed provisions.

The ties between Barbados and the thirteen colonies had always been strong, and undoubtedly some pro-American sentiment existed on the island. Aside from the commercial bonds between the two areas, many former Barbadians resided in South Carolina and Virginia, and several North American colonial legislatures in the past had been

[68] Undated. *C.O.* 29:21.
[69] Hay to Germaine, 24 October 1777. *C.O.* 28:57, nos. 1-2.
[70] Barbados, 13 April 1779. *C.O.* 30:15, no. 121.

quick to offer support and aid after the destruction of a hurricane. Governor Hay mentioned that there were "too many among these West Indians who would have been very glad to have dispersed any bad news" concerning the progress of the British army in North America.[71] In 1781 Governor Cunninghame referred to certain merchants on Barbados as favoring the American cause and maintaining connections in North America, "many of whom have been in constant correspondence and combination with the enemy".[72]

The need to trade illegally with North America was lessened early in 1778 when the Board of Trade granted a request by the West India Committee that General Howe "open the trade" of Pennsylvania, Virginia, and Maryland inasmuch as the British army and fleet was "now in possession or command of the outlets of these countries".[73] Export licenses were granted for rum and molasses to be sent "to such places as are possessed by the king's troops in any of the colonies not at the king's peace".[74] Governor Hay had his customs officers collect bonds from all shipowners whose ships left Barbados for North America to discourage additional illicit trade under the guise of supplying only areas under British control.[75]

The system appears to have worked satisfactorily for the remainder of the war. With the encouragement of the Board of Trade licenses continued to be granted by the various governors, and much of the economic pressure upon the British islands was removed by this one step. Economic circumstances had improved so noticeably on Barbados that the Assembly, after three years of pleading "famine", was reduced to petitioning for removal of the four and one-half precent tax on its exports.[76]

Throughout the spring and summer of 1778 tensions continued to build between the British and French governments over the covert

[71] Hay to Germaine, 12 October 1776. *C.O.* 28:56, nos. 79-82.

[72] Governor James Cunninghame to Germaine, 20, 23 June 1781. *C.O.* 28:58, nos. 201-207, 247, 250. In 1775 a three day celebration took place in Bridgetown over the retention by the Commisisoners of Customs of a dishonest Customs Inspector durng which Governor Hay was burned in effigy. 6 April 1775. *C.O.* 28:56, nos. 1-3.

[73] Minutes of the West India Merchants, First Series, I, 5 December 1777.

[74] Board of Trade Circular Letter, London, 10 March 1778. *C.O.* 29:22; *C.O.* 31:34.

[75] Hay to Germaine, 4 June 1778. *C.O.* 29:22.

[76] 14 April 1778. *C.O.* 31:34; *C.O.* 28:57, nos. 25-28. The Assembly was joined by the Council in this petition. They complained that the tax was being levied on the dead weight of their casks in addition to the contents. 17 April 1778. *C.O.* 31:38.

French aid given to the Americans. Hay reported that several large American privateers had come from France in recent months and were prowling the waters adjacent to Barbados and St. Vincent.[77] Prospects for war were heightened with the issuance of a confidential letter to all colonial governors by Lord Germaine in April stating that "a war with France appears to be inevitable".[78] In any conflict with France the Caribbean colonies were certain to become involved as they had been on four previous occasions. A proposal brought before the membership of the West India Merchants that the Caribbean islands be made neutral in the event that the North American rebellion were to involve other European powers was dropped for lack of a "practical" method of implementation.[79]

Rumors of war and a French attack were common. British spies reported that "the American rebel government" had been acknowledged at Martinique and that their colors flew in the harbor,[80] while Governor Hay, sensing the impending danger, attempted to force funds from his Assembly for the repair of the island's fortifications. The Assembly reacted negatively to Hay's request to reform the militia and vote the necessary taxes to provide fortification against attack; the safety of the colony had now become involved in the intra-governmental power struggle. On the eve of war with France the Assembly replied to the question of defense and new taxes with such indifference as to indicate that their failure to act was, by design, retaliation against the Governor. The statement read in part: "We must in justice to our distressed countrymen, avoid every measure of that tendency until war is actually declared."[81]

Within six months of the issuance of the Board of Trade Circular Letter opening the trade of British North America the situation of the planters had been once again drastically changed — this time for the worse. Hitherto exposed only to economic hardship, for the fifth time in eighty years the planters now stood to lose their lives as well as their possessions as soon as war with France was declared. The defenses of Barbados were grossly inadequate, the militia was disorganized and riddled with political favoritism, and finally, the ability

[77] Hay to Germaine, 27 March 1778. *C.O.* 28:57, nos. 19-20.

[78] Lord Germaine to All Colonial Governors, 1 April 1778. *C.O.* 31:34.

[79] Minutes of the West India Merchants, First Series, I, 3 March 1778.

[80] Hay to Germaine, 4 June 1778. *C.O.* 28:57, nos. 41-43. France had acknowledged the independence of the United States on 13 March 1778. Schomburgk, *op. cit.*, p. 336.

[81] Barbados Assembly to Hay, 7 July 1778, *C.O.* 31:34.

of the colony's government to function in a competent manner had been destroyed from within by bitterness and personal jealousies.

The Articles of War were published on Martinique in August, and in the British islands the following month. Within weeks Dominica had fallen to a French invasion party from Martinique, and the entire Caribbean had become a vast arena of battle once again.[82] The sea war raged intermittently with neither side able to score a major victory over the other although the recently created British privateers continued to make their presence felt by attacks upon American and French shipping throughout the Indies. Several privateers had even seized American ships within the Dutch ports and rivers of South America much to the annoyance of the Dutch who were profiting handsomely from the turn of events in the Caribbean.[83]

On Barbados, 1778 was an excellent crop year, both sugar and edible foods did well, and much of the immediate threat of privation caused by the French entry into the conflict was dissipated. But the island was now more than ever dependent upon the supply convoys from Britain to maintain itself in the face of the combined French and American threat in the Caribbean. Whether Barbados was to remain British or succumb to the power of France would depend in large measure upon the regular receipt of provisions from Great Britain, while the economic vitality of the colony rested upon the successful transportation of her sugars by these same convoys back to the mother country.[84] Without a market for sugar the colony would soon have become insolvent and worthless to the crown; as long as Barbados remained of value it would be defended regardless of the failure of its own government to rise to the occasion. This fact had become obvious to several generations of Barbados planters through four previous struggles against the power of France. It was a cushion of comfort upon which they all rested.

By 1779 the recalcitrant Assembly had begun to exhibit some earnestness in coping with the problem of the colony's security. While

[82] Dominica fell on 7 September 1778. Governor Hay reported in November that eight ships and seven thousand troops had been sent from New York by the War Office to retake the colony. Hay to Germaine, 26 November 1778. *C.O.* 28:57, nos. 65-65.

[83] *Idem.*

[84] Hay wrote of the arrival of supply convoys on several occasions: a 37 ship convoy from Cork in November 1778, 110 ships also from Ireland in April 1779, and 84 ships from London in May 1779. Hay to Germaine, 26 November 1778. *C.O.* 28:57, nos. 62-63; 28 May 1779. *C.O.* 29:22; 27 May 1779. *C.O.* 28:57, nos. 99-100.

the membership continued to stall on the matter of appropriating funds for direct defense of the island out of spite for Governor Hay, action was taken to support the military, to lessen the difficulties of supply, and to tighten the penalties against aiding the enemy. Early in the year the legislature decreed that all owners or renters of over fifty acres of land must send twenty-five pounds of meat or twelve pounds of poultry to the military yearly for each fifty acres in their possession, while the townsfolk would be required to do likewise for every £75 rent paid per annum.[85] During the same session an act to remit the tonnage duties on all provision ships entering Barbados and embargoing the export of all provisions was also passed.[86] In April all citizens were enjoined by law from corresponding with the king's enemies, and "from supplying them with provisions or warlike stores of any kind".[87]

Food prices shot upward after the French entry into the war and within six months relief flour was selling at £5 per barrel on Barbaros – a five fold increase in less than four years![88] Higher prices on most commodities reflected the increased hazards of transportation and cost of shipping, and with them the operational expenses of every plantation and business on the island. As in all inflationary times real property became the only certain protection against the loss of purchasing power, and on Barbados it remained in demand far out of proportion to its worth in relation to the production of sugar. A Barbados clergyman noting the trend wrote in 1778 that "it makes a very material difference to buy everything in these American times (as they are called here) . . .".[89] Poyer wrote that the public credit of the colony was almost annihilated as a result of inflation by 1782 even with the inclusion of a large injection of money authorized by Parliament in 1780.[90]

Militarily the year started well for the British cause with the capture of St. Lucia in January by a small invasion force, but much of the tactical importance of the capture was lost with the fall of Grenada and St. Vincent to the French soon after. In retaliation for the seizure of American ships in their harbors by British privateers,

[85] 19 January 1779. *C.O.* 30:14, no. 118.
[86] *Ibid. C.O.* 30:14, no. 119.
[87] 13 April 1779. *C.O.* 30:14, no. 121.
[88] 15 March 1779. *C.O.* 31:34. See Table V, p. 108.
[89] Letter to the Reverend Dr. Hind of the S.P.G. from a Barbados clergyman who used the pseudonym "John Codrington English". 20 July 1778.
[90] Poyer, *op. cit.*, pp. 574-576.

TABLE V

Commodity prices on Barbados, 1772–1791. Expressed in shillings

	Lumber 1000 ft.	Beef per barrel	Pork per barrel	Flour per hwt.	Cod per quintal	Herring per barrel	Corn per bushel
1772	130–190						
1773	150–190						
1774	170–200						
1774–75 average		60–70	70–100	15–25	12/6–25	25–32/6	2/6–3/9
1775	180–220						
1776		90–130	100–150	30–37/6	30–40	44–55	10–13
Oct. 1777		25*	25*	25*			
Feb. 1778						30	
March 1779				100			
May 1781				25*		45	
March 1784	150–240						
May 1784	180						
Aug. 1785	225–360	81	112/6–120	56/3–62/6	32/6	40	6/3–10
Nov. 1785	180–225	100	100–120	62/6	35	40	7/6
Jan.–Apr. 1786	141–225	85–90	90–101	47/6–50	30	37/6	6/3
Apr.–July 1786	160–240	81	80–95	47/6–50	27/6	47/6	5/7
Oct.–Dec. 1786	150–200	75	100–112/6	50	18/9	45	3/9
Jan.–May 1787	150–250	90–95	80–100	45–50	22/6–25	30–35	7/6
July 1787	180–250	85	85–100	45	17/6	37/6	6/3
1789	190–230						
1791	200–240						

* Relief Provisions.

Lumber prices for 1772-75, 1789-91 are from Edwards, *op. cit.*, p. 427n. The 1774-75 average-1776 prices are from Agent Walker's petition, *C.O.* 28:56, nos. 75-76. All others are from *C.O.* 31:34; *C.O.* 31:42; *C.O.* 28:60, nos. 257, 275, 324, 357; *C.O.* 28:61, nos. 27, 58, 142; B.T. 6:83, nos. 5. 100.

some of them from Barbaros, the Dutch began to confiscate Barbados owned property in their colony of Demerara in South America, thus hindering trade with the area and heightening tensions between the two countries at an already crucial time.[91] In July Governor Hay received permission from London to attack Spanish shipping in retaliation for numerous abuses and insults to the British crown.[92] War was about to be declared by Britain on both nations, thus enlarging the Caribbean conflict to include every European state with possessions in the Americas, save Denmark.

As bleak as the outlook regarding their ability to stave off the effects of a food shortage may have been for the Barbadians, their predicament appears to have been relatively favorable in comparison with that of the inhabitants on many of the other islands. Captured French documents revealed that French troops were suffering for lack of provisions and that many had been sent to North America with the French fleet to keep them from perishing.[93] Hay reported in September 1779, that Barbados "is the only island where they [the navy] can find provisions", and that "Antigua and St. Kitts are threatened with a famine. They have not at Antigua the wherewithal to feed their Negroes."[94]

Fighting died down in the Caribbean during 1780 after a flurry of activity during the preceding eighteen months. As if waiting and resting before renewing the battle the antagonists allowed informal warfare between the privateers to stand as their respective contributions to the struggle. British action was directly primarily against the Dutch; their possessions on the South American mainland fell before attacks by British privateers, happy to destroy profitable sources of American supplies and divert the flow of much-needed commodities to the British Islands.

The lull in fighting was accompanied by a brief lull in the political conflict between the governor and the Barbados Assembly which had gone on for the six years of the rule of Governor Hay. Late in 1779 Hay suddenly died and his place was taken by the Honorable James Dolin, President of the Council, until a successor could be appointed. Major General James Cunninghame was named to the post and arrived in Barbados in July 1780. Cunninghame was appalled at the

[91] Hay to Germaine, 27 May 1779. *C.O.* 28:57, nos. 89-90.
[92] 20 July 1779; 9 August 1779. *C.O.* 28:57, nos. 109-116.
[93] Hay to Germaine, 25 September 1779. *C.O.* 28:57, no. 121.
[94] *Idem.* See Ragatz, *op. cit.*, pp. 156-158 for details of the suffering on Antigua.

condition of the colony and immediately upon his arrival set about to rectify matters. His first move was to request funds from the Assembly to restore the island's fortifications, still in a bad state of disrepair owing to the Assembly's failure to appropriate the needed money during Governor Hay's administration.

Rather than act upon the Governor's request, the Assembly asserted its power of obstruction almost from the opening of the first session by refusing to grant the Governor his salary in full and failing to agree upon the manner in which it was to be paid.[95] Such a move was certain to renew the power struggle within the government, but the new governor proved to be more formidable adversary than his predecessor in the matter of raising money for the common defense. Sensing the futility of attempting to work with his Assembly the Governor resorted to levying a small tax on all documents issued in the course of official business as a means of raising defense funds and overcoming the deficiency in his salary.

Since a host of legal documents bearing the Governor's signature were required by practically every merchant and planter on the island in the natural course of business, the new tax directive soon created an uproar among these influential and vocal groups. Assembly reaction was direct. Claiming that Cunninghame had violated the Ancient Charter of Liberties sacred to every Englishman, by levying a tax upon writs, orders, processes, and other legal documents, the legislators petitioned the king for relief from the governor's high-handedness.[96] The Governor defended his action by claiming that the precedent for such taxes had been established by several of his predecessors, and that prices on the island were so high that in order to maintain his "dignity" he was forced to resort to extraordinary measures.[97] Within weeks of Governor Cunninghame's arrival the government of the colony had become as hopelessly ensnarled in bitterness and recrimination as it had been during the seven year term of the late Governor Hay. Until one side gave way before the other the colony would continue to drift leaderless and without direction in the face of disaster.

The most feared of all disasters struck Barbados on 10 October 1780, when after two days of steadily increasing wind and rain the

[95] Governor Hay had been paid £3,000 yearly; the 1780 Assembly voted only £2,000 yearly for Governor Cunninghame. *C.O.* 28:34, Hh. 82.

[96] Barbados Assembly to George III, 7 November 1780. *C.O.* 28:34, Hh. 66; *C.O.* 28:58, nos. 24-25.

[97] Cunninghame to Germaine, 23 November 1780. *C.O.* 28:58, nos. 26-28.

island was hit by the full force of a tropical hurricane. The devastation was almost total, not a single part of the island escaped without death and widespread destruction of property. Cunninghame reported that "Bridgetown, our capital, is now a heap of ruins".[98] Estimates of the dead and missing ran from one thousand to four thousand, many of them perishing beneath the ruins of their homes and many others having been swept out to sea.[99] Over four thousand head of cattle were lost to the storm, plus buildings valued at £350,000 sterling.[100]

The loss was so great that it would have been impossible to attempt relief measures using only the resources of the colony even if the government had been functioning properly. A general plea for aid was sent to the mother country at once, and the task of rebuilding proceeded as quickly as wartime circumstances would permit. Contingents of prisoners-of-war were hastily set to work in Bridgetown repairing the harbor facilities, while the militia and the regular troops attempted to salvage what remained of their weapons and supplies.[101]

Overseas aid was generous if not always quick. The citizens of Dublin subscribed £20,000 for the relief of the island which was used to purchase and transport provisions,[102] and the Exchequer granted £80,000 for direct relief of a similar nature.[103] Perhaps the most extraordinary and unusual attempt at relief originated near Paris in February 1781. In a letter "To all Captains and Commanders of Vessels of War" sailing in the American cause Benjamin Franklin, then American Minister to France, requested that any relief supplies from Dublin which "should by the Fortune of War fall into any of your Hands" be allowed to proceed to Barbados unmolested. In so doing, Franklin felt, the various captains would "undoubtedly recommend" themselves "to the Favor of God, of the Congress of your Employers, and of your Country".[104]

[98] Cunninghame to Germaine, 20 October 1780. *C.O.* 28:57, nos. 223-237.

[99] *Idem*; Agent Samuel Estwick to Lord Germaine, London, 22 January 1781. *C.O.* 28:58, no. 18.

[100] Estwick to Germaine, 22 January 1781. *C.O.* 28:58, no. 18. Eventually the loss was put at £1,018,928 sterling. *C.O.* 28:35, Ii. 25.

[101] Cunninghame to Germaine, 20 October 1780. *C.O.* 28:57, nos. 223-237.

[102] R. M. Martin, *The British Colonies*, IV (London, 1851), p. 115. Martin writes that when in 1847 "famine scourged Ireland, Barbados was the first among the British colonies to come forward for her relief from a public vote of £2,000, besides large contributions from private individuals," *Idem*.

[103] Germaine to Cunninghame, 4 April 1781. *C.O.* 28:58, nos. 64-67.

[104] Benjamin Franklin to All Captains and Commanders . . ., 7 February 1781. *C.O.* 28:58, no. 243.

In the midst of the united effort to recover from the effects of the October hurricane bitterness continued to grow between the Governor and the Assembly each of which was behaving in an arbitrary manner.

The Assembly finally petitioned to have the Governor recalled for his irresponsible abuse of his authority in levying unauthorized taxes. Cunninghame retaliated by dissolving the Assembly in December 1780, and relieving the colony's agent in London, Samuel Estwick, for delivering the document to Lord Germaine.[105] A second Assembly was elected and called into session by the Governor soon after, but its composition was almost identical to that of its precessor and the impasse continued into the new year.

The Dutch were the greatest losers in the military activities of 1781. Saba and St. Martins which lay north of British St. Kitts and adjacent to the notorious trading center of St. Eustatius fell to British forces early in 1781, while Demerara on the South American mainland fell to a force of privateers from Barbados and several other British islands. The hapless Dutch at Demerara were subjected to a wild orgy of plundering which lasted in sporadic fashion for several months depending only upon the whims of various sea captains and the strength of their crews.[106] Governor Cunninghame's promise to send "a proper force" to take possession of the captured colony and restore order was never carried out.[107]

The looting of Demerara would soon pale alongside the events which followed the capture by Admiral Rodney and General Vaughan of St. Eustatius in February 1781. As the principal neutral port in the Caribbean after 1778, St. Eustatius had become one vast warehouse for the storage and exchange of merchandise among the warring nations. American privateers used the island as a base of operations against the British under the protection of the Dutch flag, for a fee,

[105] 7 December 1780, January 1781. *C.O.* 31:41; 14 April 1781. *C.O.* 28:58, no. 145. Estwick was reinstated after Cunninghame's dismissal and served until 1792.

[106] Cunninghame to Germaine, 25 February 1781. *C.O.* 28:58, nos. 69-73.

[107] Cunninghame to Governor of Demerara, 18 February 1781. *C.O.* 28:58, no. 76. There is some question as to the sincerity of Cunninghame in offering to end the looting at Demerara. Schomburgk states that before war was declared the Governor had granted letters of marque against the Dutch in retaliation for Dutch seizure of Barbados assets in Demerara. Therefore we may speculate that Cunninghame had a financial interest in the sack of the Dutch colony, or (more likely) he felt that the Dutch deserved their fate in justification for their past misdeeds. Schomburgk, *op. cit.*, p. 342.

Copy

To all Captains and Commanders of Vessells of War belonging to the Thirteen United States of America, or either of them, or to any of the Citizens of the said States, or to the Allies thereof.

Passy, near Paris
Feb. 7th. 1781

Gentlemen,

It being authentically represented to me, that the worthy Citizens of Dublin, touched with the general Calamities with which Divine Providence has thought fit lately to visit the West India Islands, have charitably resolved to contribute to their Relief, by sending them some Provisions and Cloathing; and as the Principles of common Humanity require of Us to assist our fellow Creatures, tho Enemies, when distressed by the Hand of God, and by no means to Impede the Benevolence of those who Commiserate their distresses, and would alleviate them. I do hereby earnestly recommend it to You, that if the Ship or Vessell in which the said charitable Supplies will be sent to the said Islands, should by the Fortune of War fall into any of your Hands, and it shall appear to You

by

by her authentic Papers, that the Cargo is bona fide composed of such beneficent donations only, and not of Merchandize intended to be Sold for the Profit of the Shippers, you would kindly and generously permit the said Vessel to pass to the Place of her Destination; in doing of which You will not only have the present and lasting Satisfaction of having gratified your own humane and Pious feelings as Men and as Christians; but will undoubtedly recommend Yourselves to the Favor of God, of the Congress, of your Employers, and of your Country,

Wishing you Success in your Cruizes, I have the honor to be,

Gentlemen,

Your most Obedient, and most humble Servant

B. Franklin (sign'd)

Minister plenipotentiary from the united States of America to the Court of France

and while thousands starved or did without many necessities of life, the merchants of St. Eustatius grew fat with profit from trading upon the misery of others. By their unceasing pursuit of gain, the Dutch had laid up a terrible store of hatred against themselves. So high did the feeling against them run that Great Britain had declared war in 1780 largely over the question of St. Eustatius.[108]

The island was defended by a garrison numbering only fifty or sixty men when Rodney appeared off the island and demanded its surrender. The Dutch governor agreed to the demand and the colony fell without a shot.[109] The amount of material captured was almost beyond comprehension. One hundred and thirty merchant ships, plus a dozen privateers were anchored in the harbor, and Rodney wrote to his wife that "All the magazines and store-houses are filled, and even the beach covered with tocacco and sugar".[110] When the Admiral learned that a twenty-three ship convoy had departed for Amsterdam only thirty-six hours earlier, he dispatched a force to overtake it if possible and return it to the island. By fast sailing the slow convoy was soon intercepted and forced to return after brief resistance was put down; its value was later appraised in excess of £500,000.[111]

Rodney continued to fly the Dutch colors over the harbor, thus additional ships were lured into the British trap and confiscated, so that by 26 March "upwards of fifty American vessels had been taken" in this manner, plus a lesser number of ships flying the flags of Britain, France, Spain, and the Netherlands.[112] The total value of all the merchandise captured on the island and aboard the richly-laden ships was estimated to exceed £3,000,000 sterling!

British vengeance upon the inhabitants of St. Eustatius was swift and complete. All merchants were held as prisoners of war, then expelled without their property, save that which they could carry on their person. All naval stores were sent to the government shipyards at Antigua, all American and West Indian produce was convoyed to England, the town itself was destroyed and unroofed and the materials

[108] Ragatz, *op. cit.*, p. 160.

[109] J. Franklin Jameson, "St. Eustatius and the American Revolution", *The American Historical Review*, VIII (July, 1903), p. 699.

[110] *Ibid.*, p. 700.

[111] *Idem.*

[112] *Idem.* Over two thousand American seamen and merchants were captured during this operation from 3 February to 26 March 1781. *Ibid.*, p. 701.

sent to Barbados, St. Lucia, and Antigua to aid in repairing the damage caused by the recent hurricane.[113]

Rodney's greatest wrath fell upon those merchants from the neighboring British islands who had tried to keep their goods safe in case of French attack by storing them on St. Eustatius and in the expectation of immense profits had become Dutch burgers for purposes of trade.[114] To the admiral they were, "a nest of vipers, a nest of villains; they deserve scourging and they shall be scourged".[115] So great was his hatred that Rodney was willing to lay the failure of British arms in North America to their trading activities. He wrote

> I have daily experience of iniquitous practices, and the treasonable correspondence carried on by those calling themselves British merchants settled in this Dutch and the neighboring islands; and am fully convinced by intercepting hundreds of letters; that if it had not been for their treasonable correspondence and assistance, the American war must have been long since finished, nor could the French islands have been supported.[116]

In a letter to Lord Germaine, Rodney justified his harsh methods by citing the base motives of the merchants.

> We had no views whatever but doing our duty and executing His Majesty's commands, concluding the whole prize was property of the Crown; and without one selfish view thought it a duty incumbent on us, to seize for His Majesty's use all the effects of an island inhabited by rebellious Americans and their agents; disaffected British factors, who from base and lucrative motives, were the great support of the American rebellion; traitors to their king, and partricides to their country.[117]

The majority of the capture consisted of goods originating in Europe, and these – Dutch and British alike – were sold at public auction. Invitation was given and protection afforded to purchasers of all nations, and of all sorts. Under this promise of protection and clear title, British Caribbean merchants and agents representing French and American buyers flocked to the island. Never was there a better market. So great was the supply that there was little competition between bidders and lots on the average sold at one-fourth of their value.[118] An immediate result of the sale was that supplies became

[113] *Ibid.*, p. 703.

[114] *Ibid.*, p. 685.

[115] Rodney to Lady Rodney, as quoted in *Ibid.*, p. 702.

[116] Rodney to Commissioner of Customs Laforey, 27 February 1781. "Memoirs of Lord Rodney", *Naval Chronicle*, I, p. 386.

[117] Rodney to Lord Germaine, 26 June 1781. *Ibid.*, p. 386.

[118] Southey, *op. cit.*, p. 492; Jameson, *op. cit.*, as quoted in Ragatz, *op. cit.*, p. 161.

more plentiful throughout the Indies than they had been at any time since 1775.[119]

The success of the St. Eustatius expedition was met with mixed response on Barbados. Although the arrival of additional supplies was heartily welcomed, many of the merchants had lost heavily in the general confiscation of supplies. Governor Cunninghame felt that the affair "militated ... strongly against the interest of the merchants here, many of whom have been in constant correspondence and combination with the enemy."[120]

The capture of Demerara in South America proved to be of greater significance to the economy of Barbados than the various other captures made by British seapower in the Antillies. Demerara with its vast hinterland was able to furnish a host of sorely needed commodities unavailable elsewhere. Barbados trade with the captured colony expanded rapidly during 1781, and it was this trade which was primarily responsible for the adequacy of provisions on the island until the end of the war.[121]

Ominous news from North America filtered southward during the summer of 1781. A ship from Savannah brought news of the fighting between Greene and Cornwallis in the Carolinas, and another ship out of Penobscot reported the massing of French troops in Massachusetts and Rhode Island.[122] The French fleet had sailed from Martinique in late July with three divisions obviously intended for the use of Rochanbeau in New England, while Rodney remained inactive at St. Eustatius. As if in expectation of momentous events in America, activity all but ceased in the Caribbean. Cunninghame reported that he had heard the remaining French troops on Martinique and Guadeloupe were in a weakened condition physically and militarily, and that the Dutch on Surinam were in "great distress, not having had any supplies whatever from Holland since the rupture and a strict embargo having been continued there ever since".[123]

Events in North America during October forecast the end of the rebellion on terms favorable to the Americans and a return to the

[119] *Idem.* For details of the charges brought against Admiral Rodney concerning his handling of the St. Eustatius capture see Jameson, *op. cit.*, pp. 705-708.

[120] Cunninghame to Germaine, 23 June 1781. *C.O.* 28:58, nos. 247, 250.

[121] Demerara supplied Barbados with meat, limestone, tobacco, fish, salt, and Negroes, and imported from Barbados cotton, sugar, coffee, rum, and lumber (probably trans-shipped) during 1781. *C.O.* 28:59, nos. 14-16; *C.O.* 28:59, no. 35.

[122] 10 August, 27 August 1781. *C.O.* 28:58, no. 341; *C.O.* 28:59, no. 14.

[123] Cunninghame to Germaine, 18 November 1781. *C.O.* 28:59, nos. 31-32.

Caribbean by Britain and France for the final agonies in the greater contest now more than three years old. Governor Cunninghame reported the surrender of Cornwallis to General Washington at Yorktown together with intelligence of a massive French buildup on Martinique in preparation for an attack against Barbados to his Council and Assembly in late November.[124] On the basis of his information concerning French plans for an imminent invasion, the Governor proclaimed a state of emergency and tried once again to stir his Assembly into action. Barbados after six years of conflict in North America and three years of war with France, still remained almost totally defenseless against invasion. As it had done in the past, the Assembly refused to appropriate any additional funds for defense, declaring the colony "impoverished and ruined" as a result of the great hurricane thirteen months previous, and noting that

> The House of Assembly are deeply affected with the unhappy surrender of the troops under their brave general Lord Cornwallis to the superior army of the French and Americans, and are but too naturally alarmed with the Governor's other intelligence respecting the French fleet, which were so lately seen going into Martinique with the supposed disposition of the French to make an attack on this island, yet the Assembly cannot suffer their apprehensions to betray them into any means of providing for the defense of this island that are not warranted by the principles of justice or humanity.[125]

The French invasion fleet left Martinique in January 1782, headed for Barbados. Adverse winds however forced the fleet to change course and it became the fate of St. Kitts which lay eighty miles northwest of Guadeloupe to replace Barbados as the French target. The island fell after a brief fight.[126] By February 1782, only Jamaica, Barbados, and Antigua remained in British hands. Even St. Eustatius had been retaken by a French force the previous November.[127]

Governor Cunninghame had received reports early in January that the French fleet was off St. Lucia, a fact which probably indicated that a Barbados attack was about to be launched. He immediately imposed an embargo on shipping to keep any news of the British fleet's movement from reaching the French. If his Assembly was

[124] Cunninghame to Barbados Council and Assembly, 27 November 1781. *C.O.* 28:59, nos. 103-104.

[125] Barbados Assembly to Governor Cunninghame, 27, 28 November 1781. *C.O.* 28:59, nos. 105-107; *C.O.* 31:41.

[126] Schomburgk, *op. cit.*, p. 343.

[127] *Ibid.*, p. 345.

unwilling to aid in the defense of the island directly, the Governor was prepared to do everything within his power to maintain the potency of the colony's only weapon – the Royal Navy.[128] The Governor's action was greeted with a storm of protest from the planters and merchants, but the action was supported by Admiral Hood, Rodney's Second-in Command, who informed the Governor that the fleet was forming for battle and would soon attack the French.[129]

The Assembly's action in failing to appropriate funds received official condemnation from Lord Germaine, who declared that he would not have any ammunition or military stores "sent out" until the Barbadians expressed an interest in defending themselves.[130] However Cunninghame was powerless to act in face of a solid front of Assembly opposition; petitions had been sent to the Board of Trade urging his recall and the Governor had weakened his defense by his arbitrary taxation policy, which was still in effect fifteen months after its inception. The government of Barbados might have continued to function indefinitely under its handicap as it had already done for nine years, yet it was obvious that the chief losers were the people of the colony and that for the sake of efficient government a change must be made. In July 1782, Cunninghame was recalled by the Board and the selection of a successor studied.

Governor Cunninghame, like Governor Hay, had not been parochial enough in his views to suit the lawmakers of the colony. He was handicapped by his Instructions in dealing effectively with his Assembly when it acted against the best interests of the island, and he was powerless to devise alternative means of implementing needed action. When he did act in an unorthodox manner in an attempt to preserve the dignity of his office and raise funds for defense, he was censured and finally recalled.

French power increased menacingly during the winter. In early March the former Dutch colony of Demerara fell to the French, and with it a valuable source of supplies and provisions.[131] In April the Comte de Grasse fresh from his success in Yorktown six months earlier, headed with thirtyfive ships and six thousand troops toward a rendezvous with a Spanish squadron off Cuba, and then on to

[128] 5 January 1782. *C.O.* 31:42.
[129] Vice-Admiral Hood to Governor Cunninghame, 14 January 1782. *C.O.* 31:42.
[130] Germaine to Cunninghame, 6 February 1782. *C.O.* 31:42.
[131] Cunninghame to Germaine, 8 March 1782. *C.O.* 28:59, nos. 204-206.

Jamaica for an attack in force upon the richest possession in the Indies left to the British Crown.

Rodney had spent the winter of 1781–82 in England defending himself against a score of lawsuits arising from his seizure of British property on St. Eustatius and had only recently returned to the Caribbean, but when word reached the British admiral of the French move he immediately left St. Lucia in pursuit. The two fleets met near a group of tiny islands, the Saintes, situated between Dominica and Guadeloupe on 11 April 1782. In a matter of hours Rodney had achieved a victory of major proportion over his enemy: a quarter of the French fleet had been captured or sunk; DeGrasse surrendered himself with his flagship, reputed to be the largest and most powerful ship in the world; and Jamaica was spared invasion.[132]

The threat of French seapower was removed from the Caribbean by Rodney's victory at the Saintes, while in England the mood was one of peace. Although the actual signing of the first of the peace treaties was still eighteen months away, the Saintes marked the end of large scale warfare anywhere in the Americas. In London a change in the cabinet in July soon brought the war to an end on the basis of American independence. In France the government was close to bankruptcy; there was no reason to prolong the conflict. An armistice was declared in January 1783, and a peace treaty signed late in the year. The new empire had suffered a serious amputation in the loss of the thirteen colonies, and the effect of this upon the British Caribbean islands would soon become apparent.

[132] An interesting and brief account of the battle of the Saintes from the tactical viewpoint by C. S. Forester is to be found in the *American Heritage*, IX (June, 1958), pp. 4-9, 108.

VI

A NEW ERA

The events of 1783 were to prove as momentous for the British West Indies as those of 1763 had been. America, long the mainstay of the Caribbean planters and merchants as both buyer of their produce and a seller of necessities, would by the fact of its independence alone be forced into a new economic role outside the Acts of Trade regardless of its former status or commercial commitments of long standing with various parts of the British empire. The exclusion of the United States from the protective shield of the Acts however would require a reappraisal of the entire pattern of trade which had developed between the Indies and the mainland over a period of one hundred fifty years. To the exponents of mercantilism, the shipping interests of Great Britain, the American loyalists, a notable part of the British public which sympathized with them, and a majority of the Parliamentary leadership, there was no question but that a reappraisal must be made to protect the welfare of the empire and that there could be no compromise in the Acts favorable to the citizens of the new republic.[1]

Even while the Revolution raged in North America and the outcome remained in doubt, a representation submitted to the Board of Trade by a minor official of the Leeward Islands suggested that the British West Indies could be made less dependent upon America by promoting their trade with the rest of the empire – to the satisfaction and gain of all.

It must be admitted indeed that they experience many inconveniences in consequence of the rebellion; and are in want of several articles they formerly received from North America, their distress has not however been so great as was expected. It was thought by most people that they could not subsist, or at least they could not flourish without a continuance of that intercourse. In the commencement of the rebellion this was not only the

[1] Ragatz, *op. cit.*, p. 174.

> opinion of the partizans of America, but of many of the warmest friends of government. Particular articles of provisions indeed have been sometimes very scarce at Barbados, and the Leeward Islands. But that scarcity has been only periodical and might have been prevented if proper supplies had been sent out from hence. The distressed condition of most of the West Indian planters is frequently, though unjustly, urged as an argument to prove the ill consequences of the rebellion. They were greatly distressed and many of them absolutely ruined from other previous causes. But America is the scape goat and there are men who complain of being undone by the troubles in America who it is known were insolvent long before they commenced. And when the advanced price of provisions and other supplies is mentioned let it be considered how greatly the price of their produce has been advanced; nay even the rum contrary to all expectation has in most of the islands kept up to, and in others has exceeded the former price. It is contended indeed by many sensible well informed persons that there is such a necessary and immediate connection between the continent of North America and the West India islands that the latter must ever materially depend upon and follow the fate of the former. That is to be hoped not the case, but at any rate it highly becomes us to adopt such measures as may lessen, if not destroy a dependence which must be prejudicial to this country, whether we reduce America to subjection again or not. For it is not for the interest of Great Britain if she succeeds in reducing America, that trade between the continent and the islands should return to its former channel which would be established and perhaps increasing that dependence and connection which it is our policy to break as much as possible.[2]

The reversal of British military fortunes in America in 1781 gave urgency to the trade question during the twilight of the Revolution, and by 1783 agitation for the repeal of the various commercial measures designed for the thirteen colonies caused Parliament to act to exclude the United States from the benefits of the Acts of Trade.[3] The act allowed American vessels to trade with Great Britain on an unrestricted basis, but vested the king in council with the power to regulate American trade to all points within the empire as "would best promote" the interest of the crown.[4]

Three orders issued in accordance with the act set forth the conditions under which American supplies might enter British Caribbean ports. British subjects were permitted to import all kinds of lumber, livestock, grain, flour, vegetables, and bread from the United States into the islands in "British built ships owned by His Majesty's subjects". They were likewise allowed to export "rum, sugar, molasses, coffee, cocoa, ginger, and pimento . . . in British built ships owned by

[2] Unsigned, probably 1778 or 1779. Add. M. 38387 ff. 1-21.
[3] 10 March 1783. Add. M. 8133C f. 74.
[4] Acts 34-16, 23 George III, c. 39.

At the Court at St. James's, 2d of July, 1783.

P R E S E N T,

The King's moft excellent Majefty in Council.

WHEREAS by an Act of Parliament paffed this Seffion, intituled "An Act for preventing certain Inftruments "from being required from Ships belonging to the United "States of America, and to give to his Majefty, for a limited "Time, certain Powers for the better carrying on Trade and "Commerce between the Subjects of his Majefty's Dominions "and the Inhabitants of the faid United States;" it is amongft other Things enacted, That, during the Continuance of the faid Act, it fhall and may be lawful for his Majefty in Council, by Order or Orders to be iffued and publifhed from Time to Time, to give fuch Directions and to make fuch Regulations with Refpect to Duties, Drawbacks, or otherwife, for carrying on the Trade and Commerce between the People and Territories belonging to the Crown of Great Britain, and the People and Territories of the faid United States, as to his Majefty in Council fhall appear moft expedient and falutary, any Law, Ufage, or Cuftom, to the contrary, notwithftanding; his Majefty doth therefore, by and with the Advice of his Privy Council, hereby order and direct, That Pitch, Tar, Turpentine, Hemp, and Flax; Mafts, Yards, and Bowfprits; Staves, Heading, Boards, Timber, Shingles, and all other Species of Lumber; Horfes, Neat-cattle, Sheep, Hogs, Poultry, and all other Species of live Stock, and live Provifions; Peas, Beans, Potatoes, Wheat, Flour, Bread, Bifcuit, Rice, Oats, Barley, and all other Species of Grain; being the Growth or Production of any of the United States of America, may (until farther Order) be imported by Britifh Subjects in Britifh-built Ships, owned by his Majefty's Subjects and navigated according to Law, from any Port of the United States of America to any of his Majefty's Weft India Iflands; and, that Rum, Sugar, Melaffes, Coffee, Cocoa Nuts, Ginger, and Pimento, may, until farther Order, be exported by Britifh Subjects, in Britifh-built Ships, owned by his Majefty's Subjects and navigated according to Law, from any of his Majefty's Weft India Iflands to any Port or Place within the faid United States, upon Payment of the fame Duties on Exportation, and fubject to the like Rules, Regulations, Securities, and Reftrictions, as the fame Articles by Law are or may be fubject and liable to, if exported to any Britifh Colony or Plantation in America: And the Right Honourable the Lords Commiffioners of his Majefty's Treafury, and the Lords Commiffioners of the Admiralty, are to give the neceffary Directions herein, as to them may refpectively appertain.

STEPHEN COTTRELL.

Decr. 26, 1783, His majesty doth hereby order & declare that any unmanufactured goods or merchandizes, the importation of which is not prohibited by law (except oil) and any pitch tar turpentine ... being the growth or production ... may ...

A PROCLAMATION.

CLAUDE CHARLES, Vifcount de DAMAS, Marfhal of the Camps and Armies of the King, Lieutenant-General of the Government, General of the Ifland of MARTINIQUE and its Dependencies, and Commandant-General of the French Windward Iflands, in Abfence of the Governor, Lieutenant-General of faid Iflands.

JACQUES PITT, Intendant, Sieur de VIVIEGNE, Counfellor of the King and his Councils at MARTINIQUE, Prefident and Commiffary General of the Ifland of MARTINIQUE and its Dependencies, &c. &c. &c.

AS the Trade of our Colonies, and that of the Thirteen United States of North America, promifes a reciprocal Benefit and Advantage to both Nations, fo are we willing to grant the laft-mentioned every Privilege in our Ports or Harbours. In Order to animate them thereunto, it has appeared to us, as we find, that the Duty formerly ftipulated on them was not calculated agreeable to the Nature of the Trade, Lading, and Size, of their Veffels; alfo, for the Reafon of the long Detention of their Veffels in our Ports, we find that they muft have run into many unneceffary Expences, which have caufed the Lofs of their Voyage and Labour; and, to prevent thefe Obftacles, we do hereby grant and permit to their Merchants to furnifh our Colonies with every Kind of their Commodities, of which our Nation cannot fupply us with, and likewife to fuffer them to purchafe and load any Kind or Produce of our faid Iflands, of which we alfo grant the fame Privilege to our own Merchants; this being the Will and Pleafure of his Majefty, who has authorifed and ordered us to have it publifhed, and the following Articles.

ART. I. All Americans that carry on Trade in our Colonies fhall have no more Pay for every Veffel than fixteen Livres, ten Sols, Anchorage, and twenty-four Livres, fifteen Sols, at the Admiralty Office; and the fame Sum and no more to the Interpreter; for which he fhall be bound to take the Captain to the General or Governor, and to affift him in every Thing, agreeable to the Laws and Cuftoms of the Country.

ART. II. And as we want to favour, as much as poffible, the fpeedy Difpatch of all American Veffels, we do hereby permit and allow, to all their eftablifhed Merchants, to build at the Bay of Gallery a Rum Diftillery; and, round about the City of St. Pierre, proper Ciftern to keep a fufficient Quantity of Molaffes; for which we hereby exempt them free from all Duty and Tax-Money, and every one of their Negroes, for the Space of five Years.

We have thought proper to publifh, regifter, and inftitute, this at the Admiralty-Office, and every Cuftom-Houfe within our Government, and alfo charge our Director-General to ufe every Diligence to fee it executed, in Order that no Perfons hereafter may plead Ignorance.

Given in Fort Royal, Martinique, July 23, 1783, under our Seal and Coat of Arms, and the Seal of our Secretary.

Was farther figned, DAMAS and VIVIEGNE.

And, lower, by the General and Prefident,

DELEAU, DIRECTOR-GENERAL.

His Majesty's subjects and navigated according to law to . . . the . . . United States, upon payment of the same duties on exportation and subject to the like rules, and regulations . . ." as if those products were exported "to any British colony or plantation in America".[5] American vessels, on the contrary, were wholly excluded from any share in the trade, and American meat and fish were forbidden entry in the interests of pork and beef producers in Ireland and the Newfoundland fisheries.[6]

The Board of Trade felt that the remaining portions of British North America could serve as replacements for the lost thirteen colonies in the West Indian trade if encouragement was given to their residents. Nova Scotia, New Brunswick, Newfoundland, and Canada could supply the British islands with large quantities of lumber, corn, wheat, and fish, and although there might be some initial difficulty in obtaining rice and corn from these sources British shipping was of sufficient strength to transport the necessary difference to the West Indies from American ports.

The measure was a severe blow to the planters, who had hoped to enjoy a period of prosperity after the war in order that they might recover from the austerity imposed upon them through eight years of danger and privation. The exclusion of American ships from their former trade routes in the Caribbean would be certain to deprive the planters of their chief means of attaining these economic objectives, and it also raised the possibility of plunging the British islands into a trade depression unparalleled in peacetime.

In London the West India Merchants were quick to declare their opposition to any plan whereby the former American colonies would be excluded from the trade of the British West Indies. While Parliament was considering the measures which ultimately placed the United States outside the Acts of Trade, the Merchants submitted two memorials requesting a reduction in sugar duties, stricter surveillance against smuggling, and the speedy restoration of trade with America.[7]

Under a just and reasonable attention to mutual Interests, the Committee entertain no doubt but such a share of the American Trade may be preserved to the Sugar Colonies as will greatly tend to their support, and upon every principle of true Policy and proper regard to the views and purposes of

[5] St. James' Palace, 2 July 1783. *P.C.* 2:124, pp. 316-317; Ragatz, *op. cit.*, p. 180.

[6] *Idem.*

[7] Minutes of the West India Merchants, First Series, II, 11 April 1783.

rival Nations, be highly deserving of the utmost countenance and assistance from the Mother Country. To this Intercourse, the Committee apprehend, the permission of American Ships, as heretofore, freely to bring the Produce of the Dominions of the United States to the Sugar Colonies, and take back our Produce in return, is so obviously essential, that they need not adduce any further arguments in support of that proposition.[8]

The Barbados Assembly called for "our being fully restored to that free commercial intercourse with the States of America which we formerly carried on with those people under the more endearing appellation of our fellow subjects".[9] Governor Parry commented in a letter to Lord North upon one aspect of the order regulating West Indian-American trade by

observing to your Lordship that the exclusion of American lumber and horses will fall particularly hard upon this island in its present serious condition. Many curing houses and stills are rendered useless for want of horses and repairs. The American lumber and horse trade was of double advantage to the inhabitants of this island as they seldom gave anything in exchange for them but their rum, which never went to England, or at least in a very small proportion and which for want of vent, is now a mere drug upon the hands of the planters, and smuggling from the Dutch settlements upon the Main is arisen.[10]

These arguments proved to be of no avail, for the weight of logic lay with those individuals who proposed a strict adherence to the Acts of Trade. The United States was a foreign nation and according its citizens special favors could lead to the eventual domination of the West Indian trade by a rival power. Furthermore the planters might become dependent upon outsiders through this trade, thus weakening their dependence upon the mother country which bore the heavy expense of maintaining colonies in order that she alone might derive the benefits of their production. If the Americans were to profit from the maintenance of the British islands, the basis for British control over the Caribbean colonies would no longer exist.[11]

While exponents of the measure to exclude American shipping from the Indies admitted that proper enforcement of the Navigation Acts against the Americans would undoubtedly increase the cost of supplies

[8] *Ibid.*, 29 April 1783.

[9] Barbados Assembly to Governor David Parry, 27 May 1783. *C.O.* 31:41. Parry had been appointed to succeed Governor Cunninghame 31 December 1782, and arrived in the colony during the late winter. *C.O.* 28:59, no. 448.

[10] Governor Parry to Lord North, 11 November 1783. *C.O.* 28:60, nos. 68-71.

[11] John Holyroyd, Lord Sheffield, *Observations on the Commerce of the American States* (London, 1784), pp. 161-164.

and provisions in the British islands, the unnatural rise in sugar prices occasioned by the late war had left many individuals with the impression that the planters continued to reap large fortunes at the expense of the consumer and could well afford to pay a few additional pennies here and there in higher prices. The monopoly over the home market which the British planters enjoyed increased the prices of tropical produce sold in Great Britain by fifteen to thirty percent over the estimated cost of similar produce if freely imported from the foreign sugar islands.[12] To allow the planters to reap the benefits of the Acts, while they flouted their restrictions would make a mockery of mercantilism and with it the entire structure of empire.

Yet, the sudden loss of the American trade by legislative fiat was a calamity of major proportions to the West Indians, coming as it did shortly after eight years of scarcity and economic uncertainty. Parliament had artificially recreated the worst of the wartime hardships which had plagued the British planters for so long, and in so doing it was contributing greatly to a further decline in the economic health of the British island colonies.

In February, 1784, the West Indian Merchants submitted a second petition, this time to the king, requesting "free intercourse between the said sugar colonies and the United States of America in American bottoms".[13] The petition was studied by the Board of Trade which reported that when His Majesty's order of the previous July was read in the West Indies "great alarm did arise among some of the planters ... and the prices of lumber and provisions were advanced considerably beyond the ordinary course of the markets. [But] this distress was only temporary ... within the space of six weeks the price of lumber and provisions gradually fell ..."[14] The Board reiterated its belief that British shipping would be sufficient to supply the needs of the West Indies, and that the Americans unable to subsist without British manufactures would be unwilling to retaliate. The Board also noted that American trade with the French West Indies was restricted and subject to high duties in certain instances

> Upon the whole the advantages she will have in carrying on a trade with us, even under our own regulations with respect to our West Indian islands, added to those she will derive from her being supplied by our merchants

[12] *Ibid.*, pp. 187-189.

[13] 1784. *C.O.* 318:1, nos. 94-109; Board of Trade Papers (hereafter indicated as B.T.), 6:83, nos. 3-4.

[14] *Idem.*

from Europe, and the obvious disadvantage she is laid under in her intercourse with the French islands will ultimately end in her trading with us upon our own terms.[15]

Hearings on the petition continued into the spring as the Board called forth individual testimony from interested parties. Testimony delivered in March verified that American vessels were admitted into French West Indian ports and that some of the provisions which had been imported into the British islands were "introduced through the medium of the French islands ... sent thither from the American States and from thence conveyed into the British West India islands".[16] It was stated at another session that "Upon the Order in Council arriving [in Barbados], lumber which was at £7 10s. rose to £25. The price fell afterwards to £10 to £12 per 1,000 feet."[17]

The Board took note of the similarity between the economic conditions created by the king's proclamation and those created by the recent war when it attempted to determine how the islands had been supplied during the conflict. The reply was that they had been supplied "by prizes and by imports from England at a very high price – but that the high price sugar bore at that time enabled them to bear the weight; it was said also that they received some supply, in no large quantity, (of lumber) from the Floridas and from Georgia during the war."[18]

Thomas Odwyne, a member of the Barbados Council testified that lumber was selling at about £9 per 1,000 feet and that there were "no particular complaints for want of anything" on the island, but that he doubted the ability of Canada and the other British possessions in

[15] Board of Trade, 1784. Add. M. 38345 ff. 177-180. In their petition the West India Merchants had mentioned that, for lack of their accustomed rum supply, the Americans "were reduced from necessity to distill a corn spirit from their grain. But there is every reason to think from the difference in quality, and probably in price, that such spirit would not answer as a substitute, much less obtain a preference to Rum." Events were to prove the planters wrong. The tide had begun to turn from rum to whiskey during the Revolution. At the end of the war there were 2,579 *registered* distilleries in the United States, many of them using corn, wheat, or rye in place of molasses as their chief ingredient, and by 1800, rum had lost its pre-eminence among alcoholic beverages. The old diehards, the aging men who still wore small clothes and tricorn hats, might stick to rum; the new generations of drinkers took to whiskey. We can only speculate what effect the Order in Council of 1783, restricting American trade may have had in hastening this decline. *B.T.* 6:83, nos. 3-4; Stewart Holbrook, *Dreamers of the American Dream* (New York, 1957), pp. 59-60.

[16] Whitehall, 10 March 1784. *B.T.* 6:83, no. 4, pp. 7-8.

[17] Whitehall, 11 March 1784. *B.T.* 6:83, no. 5, pp. 9-16.

[18] Whitehall, 16 March 1784. *B.T.* 6:83, no. 11, pp. 35-38.

North America to serve as replacements for the thirteen colonies. He noted that "in time of profound peace, the island of Barbados usually imports about 180,000 bushels of Indian corn which is equal to about one-sixth of the consumption of the island" and that the amount was probably in excess of the entire production of British North America in any year.[19]

After several months of hearings and study the Board reported its findings to the king.

> It appears to the committee that the distress which ensued upon the publication of your majesty's aforesaid order in council was principally owing to the planters not having expected that any restrictions in this regard would take place, and having omitted therefore to make provisions of those several articles by other means.[20]

The report also noted that provision prices were continuing to fall (at least in Jamaica), and it then reiterated in detail the theory that the sugar islands could be adequately supplied from Great Britain and other portions of the empire. The Board brushed aside the threat of French competition as "inconsequential" and refused to become alarmed over the actions of the Maryland and Pennsylvania legislatures in establishing port duties for British shipping.[21]

Prices had indeed fallen throughout the Caribbean in 1784, but not because British shipping had successfully replaced American vessels on the trade routes. In the face of an order which seemed harsh and unjust the island merchants and their American counterparts had turned to the time-honored stratagem of smuggling as the chief means of satisfying their trade demands. A letter from a Jamaican merchant written in January 1784 revealed the extent of this clandestine trade between America and the West Indies. In remarking upon a fall in the price of lumber during recent weeks he wrote

> The reason assigned for the low price of lumber at Kingston is the great number of American vessels that have arrived at that port, which has occasioned a greater plenty being at market of late than was ever known before. Mr. Spreis will be able to inform you how far the Americans have been aided and abetted in carrying on the smuggling trade, notwithstanding the Governor has manifested the greatest strictness in discouraging and suppressing it. You may readily suppose that this will be extremely disgusting to that part of the community who have in the late perilous times been steady in their attachment to their king and country. At the same time

[19] Whitehall, 3 May 1784. *B.T.* 6:83, no. 100, pp. 256-261.
[20] Board of Trade to George III, 31 May 1784. *B.T.* 6:84, no. 181, pp. 151-221.
[21] *Idem.*

it is highly injurious to the fair traders who have fitted out vessels in the lumber business upon the faith of the restriction of that trade to British bottoms only. Our situation here is pretty similar to that of Kingston, for though to save appearances all American bottoms are ordered out of port, yet they have just to go round the point, out of view of the town and dispose of their cargoes. Others discharge at these bays and ports without coming near where any custom house is established. Thus they manifestly carry on their trade to a much greater advantage than before the restriction, as they are now not only freed from all custom house fees, but of whatever duties are payable on the produce they carry off. Some again take no produce, but instead of it that specie which would otherwise center in Britain, and trade with it in the French ports.[22]

Another Jamaican writing from Kingston noted that

In point of politics, we clamour loudly on this restriction on American vessels, although our ports are crowded with vessels under English colors loaded with American produce. They have overstocked our market, and at present the produce of that country sells exceedingly cheap.[23]

The writer of the Kingston letter while obviously in sympathy with the royal policy regarding trade, and while attempting to prove the wisdom of the Board of Trade's views had unwittingly exposed the extent to which the Americans had gone in their efforts to maintain their Caribbean trade: flying the Union Jack on their ships when entering British harbors. Support for this supposition comes from a third letter written from Jamaica several months after the others. Mention is made of the fraudulent use of foreign ensigns by the Americans and the collaboration of the customs officials in this subterfuge.

At present the American vessels come in under French colors and claim the benefit of the free port law, by which we get casually supplied with flour, etc., but we have no market for our rum. Some people that I know who have connections in America have written to their friends there to bring supplies as usual in American vessels saying they will protect them against the custom house. I really think that if the restraining proclamation is adhered to the whole navy of England must be employed to enforce it.[24]

Jamaica was in many ways representative of the entire British West Indies with regard to the open violation of the king's proclamation. On Barbados Governor Parry wrote

[22] Letter from John Crudon to his nephew in London. Montego Bay, Jamaica, 10 January 1784. *B.T.* 6:83, no. 40.

[23] Anonymous. Kingston, Jamaica, 19 January 1784. *B.T.* 6:83, no. 119.

[24] Extract from a letter, anonymous. Jamaica, 20 March 1784. *B.T.* 6:83, no. 60.

> Smuggling is in all these islands risen to an height ruinous to His Majesty's Revenue, the planter, and the fair trader. I have no control over the officers of His Majesty's Customs, except the power of reporting their delinquencies. I find it very difficult to stimulate them to a proper execution of their duty . . .[25]

So great was the illegal trade of St. Kitts that when Captain Horatio Nelson cleared the harbor at Basseterre of American vessels in November 1784 he was shunned by the local populace and denounced as a usurper of their trade.[26] When Nelson seized four American ships flying the Union Jack in the road of Nevis in 1785 and secured their condemnation, the local merchants prompted the American captains to sue for £4,000 damages for assault and imprisonment. Feeling on the island was so against the future victor of Trafalgar that he was obliged to remain on board ship for two months to escape being imprisoned himself.[27]

By January 1785, word of the American deceptions had reached the Board of Trade. Many United States vessels reportedly had secured British registry from dishonest customs collectors and were carrying on an extensive trade in the Caribbean unmolested by either customs or the Royal Navy.[28] The British governors were warned of this and other illegal practices, but without the support of the customs officers they remained powerless to correct the situation.[29] When Captain Ford Barnes of the Royal Navy captured a local schooner off the coast of Barbados which had been engaged in carrying on illicit trade in violation of the law, he was publicly censured by the Surveyor-General of Customs for his actions![30]

Merchants on the former neutral islands of St. Thomas and St. Eustatius continued to play their broker's roles between the Americans and the British as they had done so successfully during wartime, and since the French had thrown open their harbors to American ships in 1783, the volume of clandestine trade, unhindered by the dangers inherent in war, rose to new heights.[31]

Concurrently with the rise in smuggling activities throughout the

[25] Governor Parry to Lord North, 28 April 1784. *C.O.* 28:60, nos. 96-97.

[26] Ragatz, *op. cit.*, pp. 182-184.

[27] *Ibid.*, p. 183.

[28] January 1785. *C.O.* 28:60, nos. 221, 227.

[29] Lord Sydney to Governor Parry, 8 July 1785, *C.O.* 28:60, no. 231; 8 November 1787. *C.O.* 28:61, no. 89.

[30] Barbados, 9 January 1786. *C.O.* 28:60, nos. 299-300.

[31] Parry to Sydney, 7 September 1784. *C.O.* 28:60, nos. 182-186; 14 February 1786. *B.T.* 6:84, nos. 204-205.

Caribbean more formal efforts were being made to alter the conditions imposed by the 1783 Order in Council. The Barbados Assembly labored incessently to bring about a change in the regulations which bore down so heavily upon the colony, and in their efforts they enjoyed the full support of the Governor. Governor Parry, unlike his immediate predecessors, was a man of gentle disposition, conciliatory by nature, and in complete sympathy with the Barbadian viewpoint. Together the Governor and his lawmakers sought to alleviate the distress of their constituents by every legal means at their disposal.

As they had been forced to do in former years, the Barbadians were once again compelled to rely upon the petition as their primary means of securing favor from the crown. While the Assembly petitioned for free and open trade between Barbados and America,[32] Governor Parry, perhaps more sensitive to the realities of the complicated situation, confined his proposals to measures designed to secure temporary and limited relief for the colony. In a letter to Lord Sydney, Parry acknowledged that "open trade" would probably ruin the British merchant "who must forever be undersold by the Americans". As an alternative to this he recommended that all United States ships of one hundred tons or less carrying lumber, horses, cattle, rice, and corn be admitted to the trade of the British islands for a period of two or three years, or until such time as the provinces of British North America could supply the islands.[33] In other letters the Governor suggested that the duty on British sugar be lowered in the interest of aiding the island and to discourage the use of French brandy by British consumers; he also revieved the movement to bring a free port to the colony in order that it might create additional tax money for the crown, more employment, trade, "prosperity", and population to buy British manufactures.[34]

Parry drew attention to the fact that the Barbadians were forced to trade with Norway for naval stores and materials necessary for shipbuilding.

It is rather a bad one as we are obliged to pay with money for the stores and materials we get from thence, which will in great measure be obviated by the trade with the American states for those articles, through the medium

[32] Barbados Assembly to George III, 3 August 1784, 7 September 1784, 22 July 1785, *B.T.* 6:84, no. 196, *C.O.* 28:60, no. 187, *C.O.* 28:60, nos. 307-308.

[33] Parry to Sydney, 7 September 1784. *C.O.* 28:60, nos. 182-186; *B.T.* 6:84, no. 200.

[34] Parry to Sydney, 23 June, 7 September, 14 October 1784, 16 June 1785, 23 February 1786. *C.O.* 28:60, nos. 114-115, 182-186, 195-198, 235-246, 313-314.

of the port, where the American vessels will meet the British ships and exchange their commodities for British clothes, dry goods, etc., and the plantation rum which cannot be sent home on account of the high duty that is upon it . . .[35]

The Governor observed further that a free port would enable the Barbadians to trade more by barter and less by cash, thus upholding the mercantilistic dictum pertaining to the value of conserving coin. He predicted that merchants from the leading foreign powers would "flock" to trade

. . . and the American states being now at full liberty to choose their commercial connections, in which business the great and only directing principle, their own particular advantage, will draw to the settlement of their election, which will certainly be Barbados should it be made a free port.[36]

Finally, in a blunt attack upon the logic of the entire mercantilistic theory as it was then applied to the empire, the Governor challenged the very assumptions upon which the entire system of colonial commerce rested.

The dismemberment of the American Colonies from the British Empire, leaving them at perfect freedom to exercise their talents and improve the materials with which nature has supplied them for the purposes of commerce, has in effect estranged the Objects, and circumscribed the power of the Navigation Acts. That act (which has ever been the envy of the powers of Europe) being no longer capable of enforcing obedience to its restraints over so large a territory as it formerly controlled, the purposes for which it was passed are in a great measure defeated.[37]

Official reaction to the attempts of Governor Parry and the Assembly to gain at least a partial advantage for Barbados remained noncommittal if not openly hostile. With the weight of public and political opinion solidly behind them, government officials preferred to concentrate their efforts toward making the new regulations workable and effective. In an attempt to halt the illegal importaion of American goods into the British islands by way of the foreign West Indies an act of 1787 forbade the entry of flour, bread, rice, grain, and lumber from the islands, except that in case of emergency the Governor and Council might permit their importation for a limited time.[38]

[35] Parry to Sydney, 16 June 1785. *C.O.* 28:42, no. 64.
[36] *Idem.*
[37] *Idem.*
[38] 27 George III, c. 7; Ragatz, *op. cit.*, p. 188.

The immediate result of the new Parliamentary act was the opening of Barbados for the "emergency" importation of "flour, bread, rice, wheat, or grain of any sort, staves, shingles, or lumber".[39] Governor Parry, in a brazen violation of the intent and letter of the act, actually proceeded to throw open the colony's ports to the vessels of all nations until 1 October 1787, for the direct import and import of all commodities![40] The effect was instantaneous; the Governor noted with some satisfaction in September that "there had been more rum shipped off this island last month than there was for six months before . . ."[41] Nor was Barbados alone in making emergency importations. Dominica was thus opened twice within a year of the passage of the act, and St. Kitts and Nevis in 1789 as a result of a provision shortage there.[42]

However much individual colonies might benefit from such action the relief afforded could only be temporary. For without direct and continuous access to their sources of supply the planters would continue to suffer from the penalty attached to their monopoly of the British sugar market: compliance with the Navigation Acts. There was no reasonable basis for any other arrangement in the light of eighteenth century economic teachings, and as long as Great Britain persisted in her devotion to the cause of mercantilism.[43]

While self-interest was obviously the motivating force behind the various proposals of the West Indians for relief from the Acts, there was yet merit in much of what was proposed which only the passage of time would reveal. The British empire had sustained a loss of the first magnitude upon the North American continent, severe enough in terms of area, population, and potential, but utterly devastating in its immediate effect upon the economic balance of the empire. The forfeiture of the thirteen colonies meant the destruction of the economic equilibrium in production and consumption which formed the basis of the Acts of Trade. Without America's agricultural surpluses, her vast tracts of forest land, and her growing market, hitherto reserved for the manufactures and merchants of Britain, the Acts were only an anachronism persisting from an era forever lost at Yorktown. Without America the sugar colonies would lose the essence of their economic vitality: cheap supplies and provisions, and their foremost market.

[39] 14 July 1787. *C.O.* 28:61, nos. 74-75.
[40] *Idem.*
[41] September 1787. *C.O.* 28:61, no. 72.
[42] Ragatz, *op. cit.*, p. 188.
[43] *Ibid.*, p. 179.

The failure of Parliament to recognize fully the consequences inherent in the loss of this large portion of the empire foredoomed the British West Indies to a slow economic decay extending into the fourth decade of the nineteenth century.

As the other great trading countries of the world replaced mercantilism with a policy of freer trade among all nations the planters of the British islands began to succumb to their own inefficiences in the face of foreign competition. Canada and the other British North American possessions were wholly inadequate to serve as sources of supply for the West Indies; as late as 1790 Nova Scotia was still receiving provisions from the United States.[44] While America remained a part of the empire the inefficiencies of the British planters, fostered in part by the Acts themselves, could be borne, but once the low-cost American provisions were denied them the planters and their high priced sugars became a luxury which Great Britain could ill-afford for long.

We may argue that the West Indies were destined to lose their economic primacy within the empire to the newer tropical areas of Africa and Asia, and that continued access to the supplies and provisions of North America at the lower rate would only have prolonged the demise. Certainly that demise *was* prolonged by the great volume of illicit commerce carried on between the United States and the British islands after 1783, and the revival of higher sugar prices accompanied by scarcity of the product during the Napoleonic Wars did much to delay the effect upon the empire of America's loss. But the fact remained that the British Caribbean sugar colonies which had been nurtured under the aegis of mercantilism were incapable of survival in another economic world.

Had direct access to American supplies and provisions been granted as the West Indians requested their fate might have been different, for the volume of clandestine trade between the sugar colonies and the United States bears adequate testimony to its value to the planters.[45] A turn to a free trade pattern by Great Britain at the conclusion of the American war in 1783 would have caused an abrupt adjustment among the sugar growers as they fought to remain competitive in markets no longer reserved for their domination, yet some would have emerged

[44] Edwards, *op. cit.*, p. 421.

[45] Almost one-half of the ships (249 of 511) and one-third of the tonnage (20,587 of 68,060) entering Jamaican ports between October 1785 and October 1786 were American owned and operated. *C.O.* 318:2, no. 94.

successful — a success based upon efficiency of operation and quality of product. It would have been upon this strength that the remaining British planters would wage the fight for survival in an economic world unhindered by artificial barriers and favoritism. The denial of a free trade with the United States cost the British planters throughout the Caribbean whatever competitive edge they still possessed by 1783; it was this failure which marks the real tragedy of the American Revolution for the British sugar colonies.

Mercantilism which had given America much of its economic vitality during one hundred seventy years of colonialism was now dealt a fatal blow by American independence. The old economic system had created too well, for the very success of its creation on the North American continent was to lead ultimately to its own destruction. Just as the sugar islands had participated in the development of the imperial mercantilistic policy and had partaken of its benefits, so would they share in its eclipse. Their fate was inexorably bound to America and to mercantilism; without America to give the system life the sugar islands were economically doomed. The American Revolution cost Great Britain much of her American empire — it cost the British West Indies their economic life.

EPILOGUE

Economic demise seldom occurs quickly. Symptoms of an unhealthy state of economic affairs can be detected as early as 1650 on Barbados, and by the beginning of the eighteenth century all of the British Caribbean colonies had begun to suffer from a dislocation in their commercial relations abroad. To ascribe the islands' decline within the empire to a theory of agriculture or any particular set of economic circumstances however is to misread the evidence of two hundred years. While the British islands had the misfortune to be burdened with a unique and unhappy set of geographic and cultural liabilities, their position within the empire might have remained substantial were it not for events elsewhere.

The American Revolution can only be considered a part of the one hundred twenty five year worldwide struggle between France and Great Britain for economic and political supremacy in Europe and on the expanding frontiers of commerce across the surface of the earth. Military successes in America, India, and Europe formed the cornerstone for the expansive trade policy pursued by Great Britain throughout the nineteenth century. The acquisition of an empire was a necessary facet of that policy, both as a source of supply for the increasing industrial power of Great Britain and to furnish new markets for her manufactured goods.

An area once acquired had to be made to fit into the grand design, even if to do so might necessitate a realignment of current colonial commercial policy – even too, at the expense of other parts of the empire. It was the fate of Barbados and the other smaller British West Indian colonies to suffer from this realignment which had begun to take place on a large scale by the end of the eighteenth century. The chief product of the West Indies, sugar, had become expensive in relation to that offered by the East India Company and by additional producers in Africa. Deprived of their ready market and dependable source of supply in the United States the West Indies could only hope for legislative relief and amelioration within the Acts of Trade.

However to have remedied the situation in this manner to the satisfaction of the West Indians was an illusion, for it was the Acts themselves through which Parliament was successfully reconstructing the shape and destiny of the British Empire. The West Indies had ceased to perform their ancient economic function as energetically as several newer portions of the empire; they had become a luxury in a system organized for efficiency and profitability.

Certain palliative measures were authorized by Parliament to allieviate distress in the islands when food or other shortages arose, but these were of a temporary nature and not designed to improve the economic status of the Indies at the expense of other colonies. Indeed, this could not be done within the confines of the interlocking trade patterns so firmly established and supported in the name of mercantilism. Successful mercantilistic policy makes no allowance for sentimental exceptions to its rules. British commitment to this system was what foredoomed the West Indies to slow economic dissolution in the eighteenth and nineteenth centuries – just as this same commitment had caused these few small islands to flourish so magnificently in an earlier period.

The alternative would have been to allow the United States greater trading privileges with the empire than either Parliament or the British public was willing to give after American independence. That the Americans were accorded special advantage in their dealings with Great Britain does not mitigate the fact that this was of such a nature as to be of little value to the West Indians. There was hope in 1783 that an enlarged commercial treaty could eventually be agreed upon by the United States and Great Britain, perhaps, as Adam Smith the British economist noted, one which would lead to an alliance or union between the two nations. But the course of events would soon destroy any such hope on either side of the Atlantic.

Some debate still goes on as to whether or not the remaining portions of British North America, Canada, Nova Scotia, and Newfoundland, were able to carry out the role of replacing the United States as both supplier and customer of the British West Indies. Early nineteenth century petitions from the West Indian merchant and planter groups contain the same pleas for direct trade with the United States because of prevailing shortages and high costs as those written twenty years before. It is impossible to assess the role smuggling played after 1783, yet such evidence as we do have would indicate that it was substantial, and that the British government could not or would not (at least at the local level in the West Indies) make a concerted effort to bring it to an end. To the extent that American smuggling activities were successful, so too is the official record of support given the West Indian colonies by British North America obscured. Furthermore, after 1793 trade which had been illegal before, became more or less open and condoned as the Napoleonic Wars increased in intensity and France and Great Britain entered into their final struggle for supremacy.

This last major conflict covering a twenty year span would afford a measure of temporary economic relief for the British planters, particularly after the virtual destruction of St. Domingo by insurgent slaves early in the period, yet there was nothing surrounding the circumstances of the contest which would alter the economic philosophy of the British government with regard to the West Indies.

The hope of unrestricted free trade was soon dispelled as this privilege was merged by the Board of Trade into the mercantilistic pattern of commerce. Where free-trade ports were established in the Caribbean their purpose was to entice foreign wealth into the British orbit rather than to aid the local colonial population. The availability of free-trade ports at Jamaica, Grenada, and St. Dominica after 1784 thus served to hinder those colonies, such as Barbados, who where not so designated.

The final performance of this slowly accelerating demise would take place in 1833 with the passage of the Emancipation Act, and the following year with the freeing of all slaves throughout the British Empire. What had begun in the seventeenth century and was accentuated by the American Revolution was now completed— the ruin of the West Indian plantation economy in its original form.

The primary cause of it all had been the failure to reestablish trade relations with the thirteen mainland colonies after they became the United States. There were good reasons for not doing so in 1783, and from the perspective which history affords the decisions of 1783 seem even more correct for the benefit which they accorded the empire as a whole in the ensuing years. The United States was the natural trading partner for the sugar colonies of the Caribbean; here was a complimentary relationship which could not be duplicated. Without access to American supplies the British islands were destined to economic indigence unless their value to the mother country could be restored to that of an earlier period. But the virgin soils of newer portions of the empire could outproduce and thus undersell the sugar products of the British West Indies on the London market, effectively removing the last hope of relief from the oppressive burden placed upon the West Indians.

The world had changed too swiftly for the West Indians to keep pace. Yet, considering the factors of size, distance, wealth, and population perhaps they had done more than might have been expected to extend British power and influence in the New World for two hundred years?

BIBLIOGRAPHY

PRIMARY DOCUMENTS, UNPUBLISHED

Colonial Office Papers; Board of Trade Papers; Calendar of State Papers.
These documents pertaining to the West Indies constitute the principal sources of information used in compiling this work. All are available at the Public Record Office, Chancery Lane, London, W.C.2. Material prior to 1736 is available in printed form as the Calendar of State Papers, all other documents are found in the original.

British Museum Manuscripts.
Material on the West Indies is available in original form in the Manuscript Room of the British Museum. Many of the trade statistics for the work were located in the British Museum.

Society for the Propagation of the Gospel Papers.
Letters from various clergymen and laymen written to the Society are kept in the Society's archives, 15 Tufton Street, London, W.2. Much of the material pertains to church affairs, yet occasional references to secular events make a search of the papers most rewarding. The letters and documents are incomplete and not well indexed; most are kept in loose order in large boxes each of which may span a ten or twenty year period.

West India Committee Archives.
The minute books of the West India Merchants and its successors from April 1769, are available in two volumes at the Committee's library, 1 Norfolk Street, London, W.C.2. The activities of this influential group are easily traced through the minutes of their meetings and are of great value in any study of planter reaction to the Acts of Trade.

SECONDARY WORKS

Beer, George L., *British Colonial Policy, 1754-1765* (New York, 1933).
A detailed study of the Seven Year's War and its aftermath by one of the foremost American historians of the colonial period.

Burn, W. L., *The British West Indies* (London, 1951).
A good survey of political, social, and economic British West Indian history. Has a full discussion of the value of sugar to Great Britain in the eighteenth century and the 1763 debate over the retention of the French islands.

Burns, Sir Alan, *History of the British West Indies* (London, 1954).
A well documented text; primarily a political history of the British islands. Emphasizes the planters' economic struggle against trade restrictions and foreign sugar competition.

Campbell, Dr. John, *Candid and Impartial Considerations on the Nature of the Sugar Trade* (London, 1763).
A treatise on the value of retaining Martinique and Guadeloupe after the Seven Year's War.

Churchill, Winston, *History of the English Speaking Peoples,* III (London, 1957).

Edwards, Bryan, *The History, Civil and Commercial, of the British Colonies in the West Indies* (London, 1793).
A two volume work on the British West Indies. Primarily a political history, but suitable as a research tool for the student of economic and social history because of its size and breadth.

Frere, George, *A Short History of Barbados* (London, 1768).
Another of the quasi-historical works of the mid-eighteenth century by a writer favorable to the West Indian viewpoint.

Hall, Douglas, "The West India Committee, A Historical Outline", unpublished MSS (London, 1956).
A well-written study of the West India Committee and its precursors based upon a thorough examination of the archives of the organization.

Harlow, V. T., *A History of Barbados, 1625-1685* (Oxford, 1926).

Holbrook, Stewart, *Dreamers of the American Dream* (New York, 1957).

Holroyd, John, Lord Sheffield, *Observations on the Commerce of the American States* (London, 1784).
An economic treatise on the importance of maintaining the force of the Navigation Acts after the loss of the thirteen colonies by the foremost proponent of this view. Affords the reader a summation of what became official policy with regard to the United States after the Revolution.

Makinson, D. H., "A Survey of the Barbados Sugar Industry, 1642-1764", unpublished MSS (Iowa City, 1959).

Martin, R. M., *The British Colonies,* IV (London, 1851).

Mauduit, Israel, *Considerations on the Present German War* (London, 1761).
Contains references to the value of Guadeloupe and Martinique to the British empire.

Morison, Samuel E. and Commager, Henry S., *The Growth of the American Republic,* I (New York, 1942).

Namier, Sir Lewis, *The Structure of Politics at the Accession of George III* (London, 1929).
A detailed study of the composition of the government during the crucial period of the Seven Years' War.

Osborne, T., *Caribbeana, Letters and Dissertations* (London, 1741).

Pares, Richard, *Colonial Blockade and Neutral Rights, 1739-1763* (Oxford, 1938).

—, *Yankees and Creoles* (Cambridge, 1956).
A well written study of the trade between the inhabitants of the West Indies and the North American colonists during the seventeenth and eighteenth centuries. Includes several charts and diagrams on the volume of trade and a good description of the economic factors involved in ocean commerce.

Parry, J. H. and Sherlock, P. M., *A Short History of the West Indies* (London, 1957).
A comprehensive political and economic history of the West Indies up to the modern period.

Penson, Dame Lillian, *The Colonial Agents of the British West Indies* (London, 1924).
Contains a good history of the West India Committee in addition to a detailed description of the workings of the Board of Trade during the eighteenth century.

Pitman, F. W., *The Development of the British West Indies* (New Haven, 1917).
Gives a good account of the economic developments in the eighteenth century prior to the Treaty of Paris. Also shows the results of seventeenth century economic policies upon the sugar trade.

Poyer, John, *The History of Barbados, 1605-1801* (London, 1808).
A political history of Barbados. Reads easily, but most of the statements and conclusions are either poorly documented or without documentation. Neither more or less useful than the other works of the period.

Ragatz, Lowell J., *The Fall of the Planter Class in the British Caribbean, 1763-1833* (London, 1928)
A classic study of West Indian social and economic history from the Treaty of Paris to the Emancipation Act of 1833. Written in a clear, concise style, the book is perhaps the most complete study ever undertaken of this period. While no attempt has been made to focus the study upon any colony or group of colonies much of the material pertains to Jamaica, therefore students of the other British islands may find much of the presentation incomplete. As a general history of the British West Indies for the period described it is unsurpassed.

Schomburgk, R. H., *The History of Barbados* (London, 1848).
A nineteenth century classic covering such diverse subjects as climatology and meteorological phenomena, animal and bird life, and political history to 1846. One of the better secondary resources for students of eighteenth century colonial, political and economic life.

Southey, Captain Thomas, *Chronological History of the West Indies,* II (London, 1827).

ARTICLES

"Memoirs of Lord Rodney", *Naval Chronicle*, I.

Forester, C. S., "The Battle of the Saintes", *American Heritage*, IX, pp. 4-9, 108.

Jameson, J. Franklin, "St. Eustatius in the American Revolution", *American Historical Review*, VIII, pp. 683-708.

INDEX